Traditional Aboriginal Lands

Tutchone

Tlingit

Tagish

Inland Tlingit (Taku)

Kaska

Dene-thah

Tahltan

Sekani

Dunne-za

Nisga'a

Gitxsan

Haida

Saulteux, Cree

Tsimshian

Wet'suwet'en

Haisla

Dakelh

Heiltsuk

Nuxalk

Tsilhqot'in

Secwepemc

Oweekeno

Kwakwaka'wakw

Homalco

Stl'atl'imc

Klahoose

Sliammon

Nlaka'pamux

Okanagan

Ktunaxa, Kinbasket

Nuu-chah-nulth

Qualicum

Sechelt

Squamish

Stó:lō

Snuneymuxw

Cowichan

Ditidaht

Semiahmoo

Tsleil Waututh

Musqueam

Tsawwassen

Saanich

Lekwammen

T'sou-ke

Esquimalt

North

West — East

South

0 50 100 150 200
kilometres

Our Communities

OUTLOOKS **3**

SHARON
STERLING

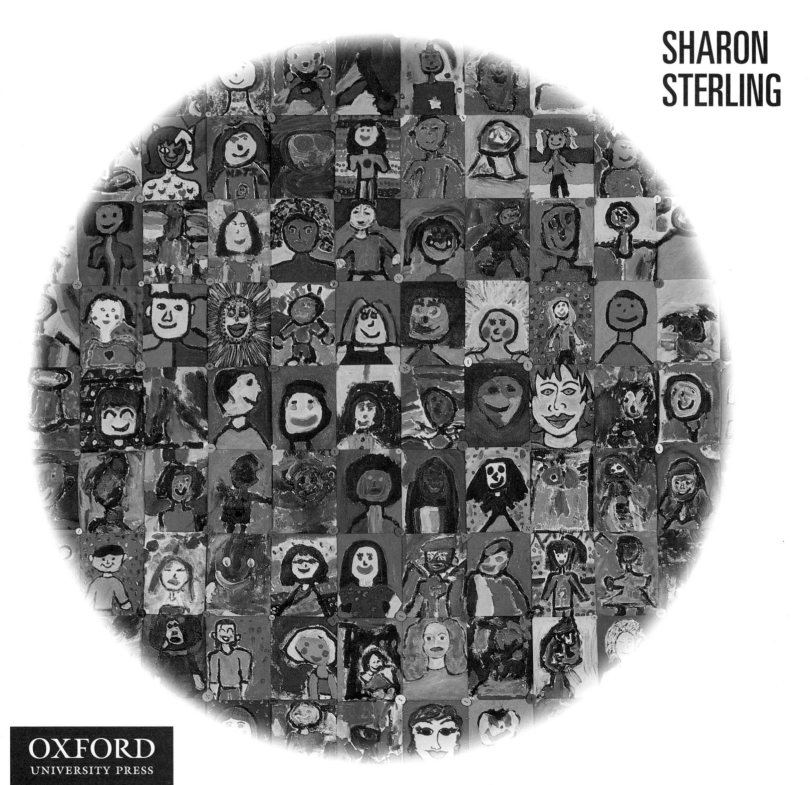

OXFORD
UNIVERSITY PRESS

OXFORD
UNIVERSITY PRESS

70 Wynford Drive, Don Mills, Ontario M3C 1J9
www.oup.com/ca

Oxford University Press is a department of the University of Oxford.
It furthers the University's objective of excellence in research, scholarship,
and education by publishing worldwide in

Oxford   New York
Auckland   Bangkok   Buenos Aires   Cape Town   Chennai   Dar es Salaam   Delhi
Hong Kong   Istanbul   Karachi   Kolkata   Kuala Lumpur   Madrid   Melbourne
Mexico City   Mumbai   Nairobi   São Paulo   Shanghai   Singapore   Taipei   Tokyo   Toronto

and an associated company in Berlin

Published in Canada
by Oxford University Press

National Library of Canada Cataloguing in Publication Data

Sterling, Sharon, 1955-
    Our communities

(Outlooks; 3)
For use in Grade 3, in British Columbia.
Includes index.
ISBN 0-19-541549-3

1. Community—Juvenile literature. I. Title. II. Series.

LB1584.5.C3S72 2002   307   C2001-904204-3

2 3 4 – 05 04 03 02

This book is printed on permanent (acid-free) paper. ∞

Printed in Canada

Acquisitions Editor: Marian Marsh
Developmental Editor: Linda Biesenthal
Copy editor: Kathy Vanderlinden
Cover and text design: Brett Miller
Cartographic and technical art: Paul Sneath / free&creative
Illustrations: Dale Adams
Art pages 92 and 93: Shana Schwentner
Text formatting: PageWave Graphics Inc.

Contents

Introduction

Our Communities is a social studies textbook. Social studies is about the people and places in the world around you.

This year in social studies, you can explore your own community and find out about other communities. You can learn interesting things, such as where electricity comes from, how money works, and why the beaver is a symbol of Canada. You can also learn important things, such as how your words and actions can help make the world a better place.

Best of all, social studies is fun! The pictures on these pages show you some of the things you might do in social studies this year.

CHAPTER 1

DOING YOUR PART

One way to find out about the world is to be curious and ask questions! In social studies, questions get you thinking about what you know and what you want to find out.

In this book, every chapter starts with a Big Question. Here is the Big Question for this chapter: *How can you help make your community a friendly and safe place?*

The rest of this chapter has information to help you answer the Big Question. You can read about
- what makes a community friendly and safe
- your rights and responsibilities

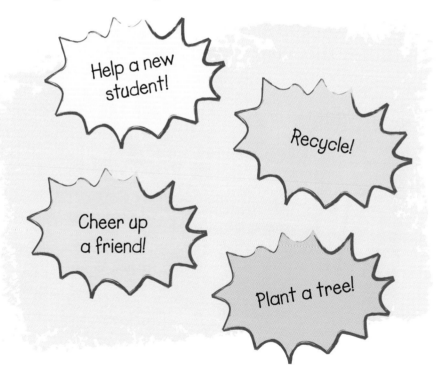

Help a new student!

Recycle!

Cheer up a friend!

Plant a tree!

▲ Small actions make a big difference. How could these actions make your community a friendly and safe place? What other actions can you think of?

Friendly and Safe

Before you read, preview to find out where this section begins and ends. Look at the headings and pictures to see what it is about.

READING HINT

A classroom or school is like a small community. You might already have some ideas about what makes a classroom friendly and safe. See if you agree with the ideas on these pages.

Friendly Communities

In a friendly community, everyone feels welcome. Nobody is left out, and people help each other.

When there is work to be done, each person does a part. When it's time to have fun, everyone joins in.

◀ Do you think these students are working together in a friendly way? What makes you think that? What do you do to make your classroom a friendly place?

Safe Communities

In a safe community, people follow rules when they are working and playing. That helps make sure nobody gets hurt. When people have problems getting along, they work it out by talking, not by hitting or shouting.

Safe communities are also clean and healthy places to live. People get rid of garbage and recycle to help keep the land, air, and water clean.

◄ What safety rules are these students following? What other safety rules do you know?

YOUR TURN

Make a picture to show your idea of what a friendly and safe community would look like, sound like, and feel like. You could show your class, your school, or the street where you live.

Rights and Responsibilities

READING HINT

If a word is in bold (**like this**), it is important. If you need help to know how to say the word, check the glossary on pages 150–151.

People need to work together to make their communities friendly and safe. The job is easier if all the members of a community understand their rights and responsibilities. That includes you!

You have four important kinds of **responsibilities** in your community.

Be . . .

Helpful • Do your share of the work and help others when you can.

Peaceful • When problems come up, work to solve them in peaceful ways.

Respectful • Treat others the way you would like to be treated.

Caring • Do what you can to make your school, your community, and the world a better place.

What about your **rights**? If you act responsibly, then you have the right to be treated well by other people. For example, you have the right to get help when you need it and the right to be treated with respect.

Writing It Down

Sometimes people write down their rights and responsibilities to make sure everyone agrees.

Here are three of the rights and responsibilities that some students decided were important in their class. What do you notice about how rights and responsibilities are matched?

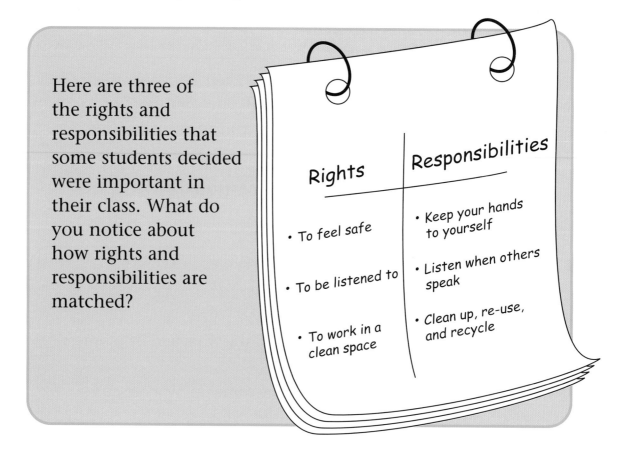

Rights	Responsibilities
• To feel safe	• Keep your hands to yourself
• To be listened to	• Listen when others speak
• To work in a clean space	• Clean up, re-use, and recycle

YOUR TURN

1. Work together to decide on a list of rights and responsibilities for your class. Think about being helpful, peaceful, respectful, and caring.

2. Look over your list. Think of one way you could use these same ideas in your community.

Choose an Idea

In our classrooms and communities, we often work with others to solve problems or get things done. Here are some steps that can help you come up with good ideas.

1. Describe what the problem is or what needs to get done.

2. Brainstorm ideas. Include every idea you can think of.

3. Look back and circle the idea you think will work best.

4. Think it through. Ask these questions:
   - What makes this a good idea (pluses)?
   - What might cause problems (minuses)?
   - Can we solve the problems? How?

5. If it still looks like a good idea, try it out.

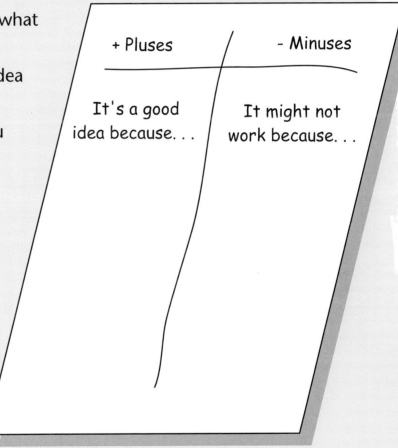

+ Pluses	- Minuses
It's a good idea because. . .	It might not work because. . .

▲ Making a chart can help you sort out the pluses and minuses.

Look again at these pictures and ideas from Chapter 1. Then decide how you would answer the Big Question: *How can you help make your community a friendly and safe place?*

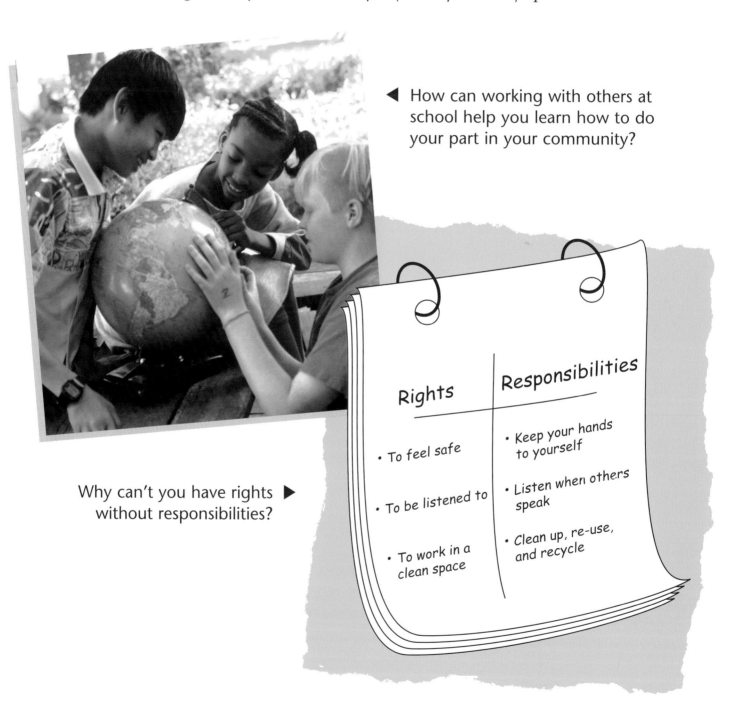

◄ How can working with others at school help you learn how to do your part in your community?

Why can't you have rights ► without responsibilities?

Rights	Responsibilities
• To feel safe	• Keep your hands to yourself
• To be listened to	• Listen when others speak
• To work in a clean space	• Clean up, re-use, and recycle

CHAPTER 2

BC COMMUNITIES

Where is your community? Is it near the ocean or by a river? Is it in the mountains or in the middle of flat grasslands?

You can find communities in all these kinds of places in BC. BC is short for British Columbia. British Columbia is the name of the province where you live.

The Big Question for this chapter is: *What are some interesting sites to see and communities to visit in British Columbia?* To help you answer this question, you can

- look at maps of British Columbia
- read about the first people to live in British Columbia
- read reports on three BC communities

▲ This picture was done by a student in Abbotsford, BC. What does it show you about Abbotsford? What would you show in a picture of your community?

BC: Physical Features

READING HINT

This map shows **physical features**. Look for landforms and water bodies, such as mountains, rivers, and lakes.

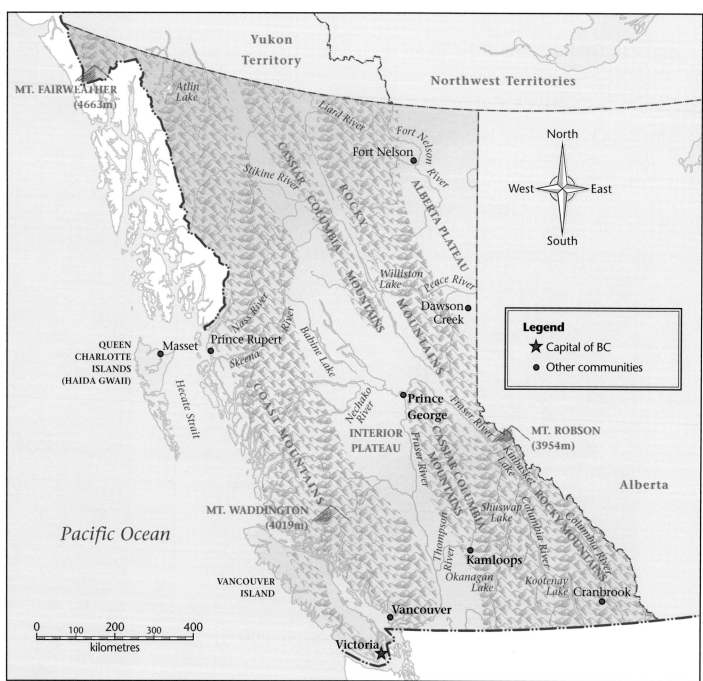

YOUR TURN

These photographs show four physical features in BC. Find these places on the map. Decide which one you would like to visit.

▲ The Rocky Mountains are on the east side of BC.

▲ The Fraser River flows through the southern part of BC.

▲ This is a beach on the Queen Charlotte Islands.

▲ The Interior Plateau is east of the Coast Mountains.

Aboriginal Peoples

READING HINT

A sidebar gives you extra information or asks questions to get you thinking. The sidebar in this section tells you the meaning of an important word.

Aboriginal peoples lived in British Columbia before anyone else. They made their homes in all parts of the province.

There are many different Aboriginal groups. Some groups share the same language and traditions. Other groups have different languages and traditions.

Traditions are ideas and ways of doing things that are passed on from adults to children in families and communities.

Each group has traditional lands in a different part of British Columbia. Today, Aboriginal people live anywhere they choose, but their traditions and lands are still important to them.

Every year people from many ▶ different Aboriginal groups come together to celebrate their traditions at the First Peoples Festival in Victoria, BC.

YOUR TURN

Make a map that shows where your community is in British Columbia. Also show the traditional Aboriginal lands it is part of.

There are two maps inside the front cover of this book. They can give you the information you need to make your map.

- The BC Communities map shows communities in British Columbia. You can use this map to find your community or a community close to it.
- The Traditional Aboriginal Lands map shows the traditional lands of different Aboriginal groups in British Columbia. You can use this map to find out which traditional lands your community is part of.

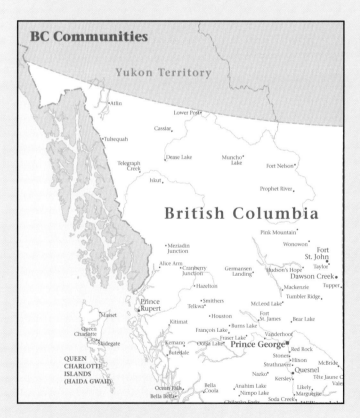

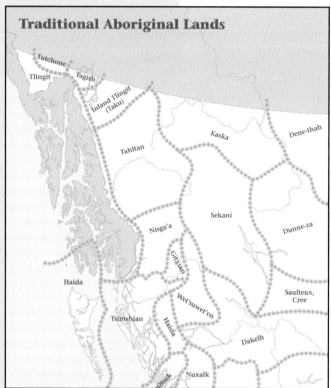

Three Communities

READING HINT

Notice the information in brackets after the community name "Ahousat." This shows you how to say the word.

This section includes reports on Ahousat [a-HOWZ-it], Fort Nelson, and Kelowna. These communities are in different parts of British Columbia.

These reports can give you an idea of some sites to see and communities to visit in British Columbia. They can also show you how to describe a community.

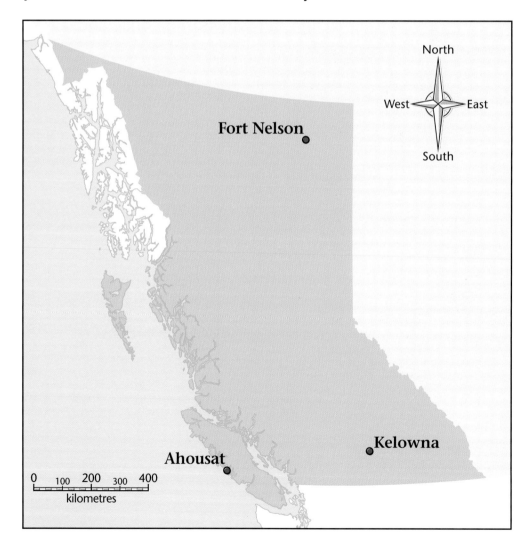

Describing a Community

There are three kinds of facts that can help describe a community: **population**, **location**, and **environment**.

A community's population, location, and environment are important. They are important because they make a difference to what people can do for work and play in their communities.

▲ When you read the reports on Ahousat, Fort Nelson, and Kelowna, look for headings that match the ones in this web.

Ahousat

Population

900 people

Location

Ahousat is on Flores Island. This is a small island near Tofino on Vancouver Island. Ahousat is in the traditional lands of the Nuu-chah-nulth [noo-CHAH-noolth].

Environment

Flores Island is surrounded by the Pacific Ocean. The island has forests of sitka spruce and sandy beaches. The area gets a lot of rain. Winters are cool. Summers are warm.

▲ Sitka spruce are evergreen trees. They have needles instead of leaves and stay green all winter.

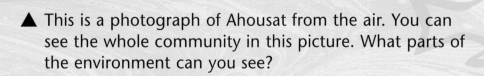

▲ This is a photograph of Ahousat from the air. You can see the whole community in this picture. What parts of the environment can you see?

Community Life

Fishing is the main kind ▶ of work in Ahousat. How can you tell these are fishing boats?

▲ The Ahousat general store sells things that people need. Look at the signs on the front of the store. What else can you do there?

▲ On School Beach Day, people in the community come together to picnic and play games at the beach.

Fort Nelson

Population

4401 people

Location

Fort Nelson is in the far north of British Columbia, on the east side of the Rocky Mountains. This area is part of the traditional lands of the Dene-thah [de-ney-TA].

Environment

The land around Fort Nelson is quite flat, with some low hills. There are forests and many lakes and rivers. Fort Nelson has cold, snowy winters and cool summers.

▲ There are a lot of wild animals in the forests near Fort Nelson. If you go for a drive, you might see elk!

▲ This shows the Alaska Highway going through Fort Nelson. What can you tell about the environment from this photograph? What can you tell about the community?

Community Life

People who live in Fort Nelson like to canoe on the ▶ lakes and rivers. Tourists come to the area to see the scenery and wildlife. How can tourism make jobs for people in the community?

▲ There is a lot of natural gas in the ground near Fort Nelson. Many people work in this plant to make the gas into fuel for heating and cooking.

In January, there is a famous dogsled ▶ race in Fort Nelson. What do you think it sounds like when all the dogs are getting ready to run?

Kelowna

Population

89 442 people

Location

Kelowna is in the Okanagan Valley, beside Okanagan Lake. The Okanagan Valley is in the traditional lands of the Okanagan Nation. Kelowna means "grizzly bear" in their language.

Environment

There are low hills around Kelowna. Most of the area is grassland with some trees. The rich soil is good for growing fruits and vegetables. Kelowna gets cold, dry winters and sunny, hot summers.

▲ Fruit trees grow best in places that get a lot of sunshine.

▲ This photograph of part of Kelowna was taken from the air. What in this picture shows you Kelowna is a big city?

Community Life

In downtown Kelowna, ▶ there are many stores, restaurants, and offices.

◀ This is an orchard—a kind of farm where fruit is grown. Growing fruit is one of the main types of work around Kelowna. Why is the environment near Kelowna so good for orchards?

Okanagan Lake is a favourite ▶ spot for recreation in the summer. What can you do for fun if you live near a lake?

YOUR TURN

Pick one community in British Columbia that you'd like to visit. Make a postcard you could send to a friend. You can choose Ahousat, Fort Nelson, Kelowna, or another place you know about.

◀ On the front of your postcard, show something special about the location or the environment.

Wheat fields near Dawson Creek

August 10th

Hi, Simma!

Here I am in Dawson Creek. It is in the Peace River area. They grow a lot of wheat here. Today I rode on a tractor!

 Love, Julie

Simma Alvay
General Delivery
Likely, BC
V0L 1N0

◀ On the back of your postcard, describe what the picture shows. Then write a few sentences about what you would do if you visited this community.

Find Information

1. Before you start looking for information, decide how you will record it. You might make a chart like this one.

Topic: Prince Rupert		
My Questions	What I Found Out	Where I Found It
Where is it?	On Kaien Island, where the Skeena River meets the Pacific Ocean	Class map of BC
What is the population?	16 620 people	Welcome to Prince Rupert Web site

2. Look for information in different places. Books, computer programs, Web sites, and people are all good sources of information.

3. When you look for information in books, use skimming to help you save time. If you find the answer to one of the questions, mark the spot with your finger. Then write down the information.

4. When you think you are finished, check your chart to make sure you have answered all your questions. You might find you have new questions to add.

Skimming
To skim, don't read every word. Read the headings and the first sentence or two of each paragraph. Also look at the pictures.

Look again at these pictures and ideas from Chapter 2. Then decide how you would answer the Big Question: *What are some interesting sites to see and communities to visit in British Columbia?*

◀ What are physical features?

What did you learn about traditional Aboriginal lands in British Columbia? ▶

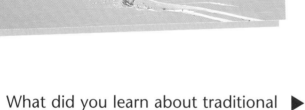

Environment
• Land, water, air, weather, plants, and animals

◀ Give one example of how the environment makes a difference in what people do for work or play in their communities.

CHAPTER 3

YOUR COMMUNITY

Your community is a busy and interesting place!

It takes a lot of work to make sure people in your community get what they need. Some workers provide **services** that help keep the community healthy and safe. Other workers make sure there are **utilities**, such as electricity and water.

People also need different kinds of places in their communities. If you look around your community, you might see places to live, places to shop, and places to have fun.

The Big Question for this chapter is: *What kinds of services, utilities, and places do you have in your community?* To help you answer this question, you can
- read information on services and utilities
- look at photographs of a neighbourhood in Vancouver
- find out how to make a map of your neighbourhood

Community Services

READING HINT

Pause and think after each paragraph. If you are not sure what the main idea is, read the first sentence again. It usually tells you.

There are two main kinds of community services: everyday services and emergency services.

Everyday Services

Everyday services give us the things we need all the time. They are like the chores we do at home. Changing a light bulb and taking out the garbage might not seem very important. But doing these chores keeps our homes safe and healthy.

▲ Here are two everyday services. How do they help keep the community safe and healthy?

Emergency Services

Emergency services help us when we have problems.

People who work in emergency services also help make sure we don't have emergencies. For example, police officers might come to your school to tell you about traffic safety rules.

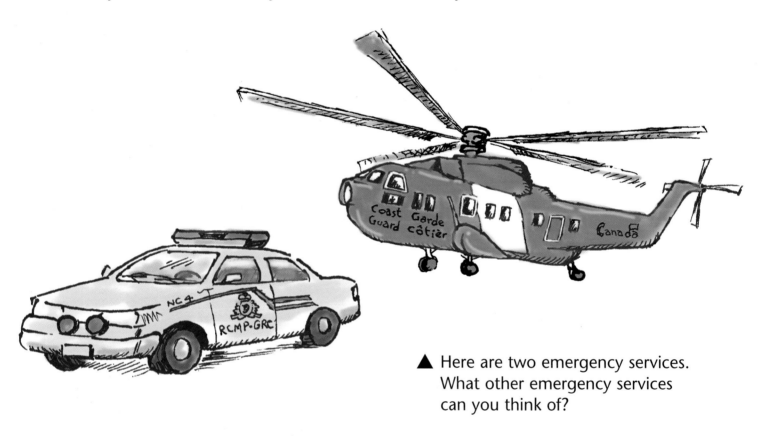

▲ Here are two emergency services. What other emergency services can you think of?

YOUR TURN

1. Do some research to find out about the everyday and emergency services in your community.

2. Pick one service. Write a thank-you letter to the workers who provide the service. Tell them why what they do is important to the people in your community.

Utilities

READING HINT

Notice how this section is organized. It starts with main ideas about utilities. Then it gives details about one utility: electricity.

Utilities are the useful things that usually come into our homes through wires, cables, or pipes. Here are examples of utilities that many people in British Columbia have in their homes.

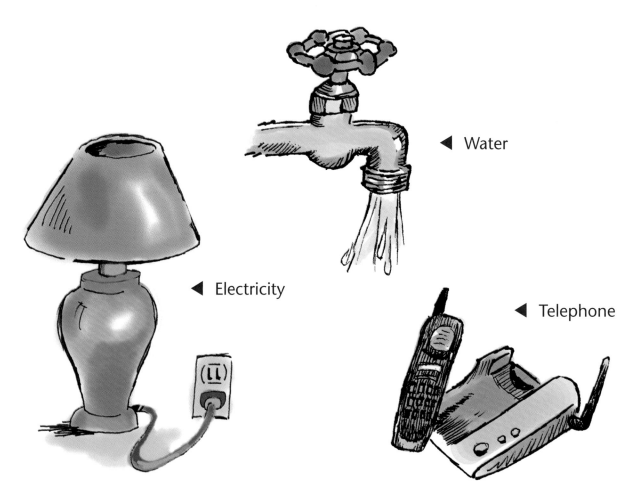

◄ Water

◄ Electricity

◄ Telephone

People might get these utilities in different ways. For example, most people who live in cities get their water through pipes from someplace far away. Many people who live in the country get their water from wells on their properties.

Looking at Electricity

It takes a lot of work to make and deliver utilities. Follow these steps to find out what it takes for you to be able to turn on a light!

1. Making Electricity

One way to make electricity is to use water. This is done at a hydroelectric dam.

In this kind of dam, the water from a river rushes over a turbine. A turbine is round like a wheel. As the water goes past it, the turbine spins faster and faster. This spinning makes energy that is turned into electricity.

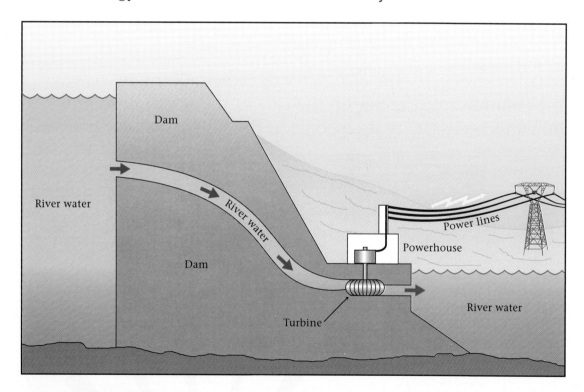

▲ Workers at hydroelectric dams make sure the right amount of water is going over the turbines.

2. Power Lines

Thick wires carry the electricity from the dam to power stations near communities.

Crews of ▶
workers build
new lines and
repair old ones.

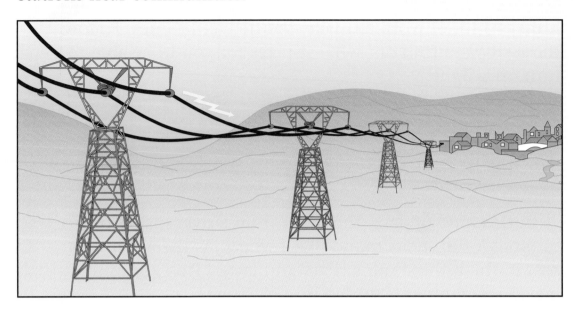

3. Electricity in Our Communities

Smaller wires carry the electricity to each building in the community. A meter on the side of the building records how much electricity the people in the building use.

Someone from ▶
the electricity
company reads
the meter to see
what people
have to pay for
their electricity.

YOUR TURN

1. Use the drawings in "Looking at Electricity" to explain to a partner how electricity is made from water and how it gets to buildings in a community.

2. Make a web that shows some of the things in your home or school that need electricity to work. Here are some pictures to help get you thinking.

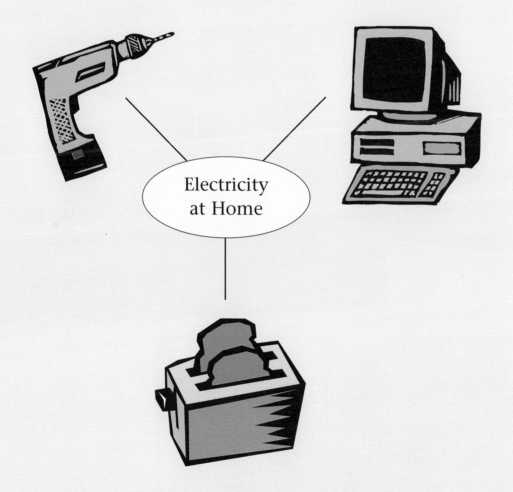

Electricity at Home

▲ The pictures used in this web are called clip art. You can get pictures like these from a file on a computer. If you have a computer, you might be able to use clip art in your web.

Mount Pleasant

READING HINT

When you look at each photograph in this section, ask yourself: What kind of place does this show? Why do communities need places like this?

People need services and utilities in their communities. They also need different kinds of places. This section shows you some of the places in the Mount Pleasant neighbourhood in the city of Vancouver.

YOUR TURN

Use lists to help you compare the Mount Pleasant neighbourhood to your neighbourhood.

1. First, make a list of all the kinds of places in Mount Pleasant that you can see in the photographs.

Mount Pleasant
- places to shop
- homes

Our Neighbourhood
- homes
- boat dock

2. Next, make a list of the kinds of places your neighbourhood has. If you live in a small town, the whole community might be your neighbourhood.

3. Now put your lists beside each other and underline the things that are the same.

Mount Pleasant
- places to shop
- homes

Our Neighbourhood
- homes
- boat dock

4. Think about the things that are the same in the lists you made. Do you think you would find these kinds of places in other neighbourhoods? Why?

Maps

READING HINT

Before you read this section, think of what you already know about maps. Where have you seen maps before in this book?

If you wanted to tell somebody about your neighbourhood, it would help to have a map to show where all the places are.

A map shows what you would see if you were a bird flying over a place. Here is a map of Kayla's backyard.

What a Bird Would See

The Map

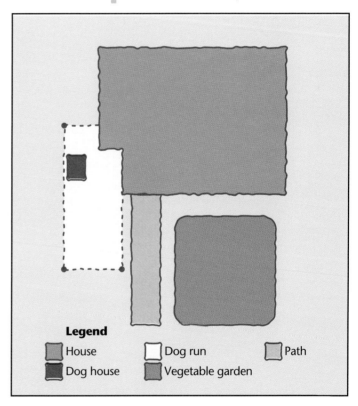

Legend

House   Dog run   Path

Dog house   Vegetable garden

▲ Which parts are the same in the map and the drawing? Which are different?

Make a Map

Here are some features to include when you make a map.

Symbols

Use colours, shapes, and lines to stand for things such as roads, buildings, and lakes. Special shapes and lines are called **symbols**.

Legend

Make a **legend**. A legend is a list of the symbols on a map. It might also show what the colours on the map stand for.

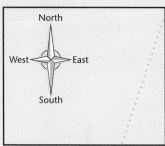

Compass Rose

Include a **compass rose**. This shows the directions north, south, east, and west.

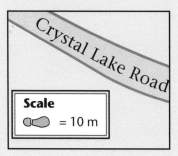

Scale

A map is smaller than the place it shows. Include a **scale** to show the size things really are.

YOUR TURN

Here is a map of the Shady Creek neighbourhood.
Use the map to answer the questions.

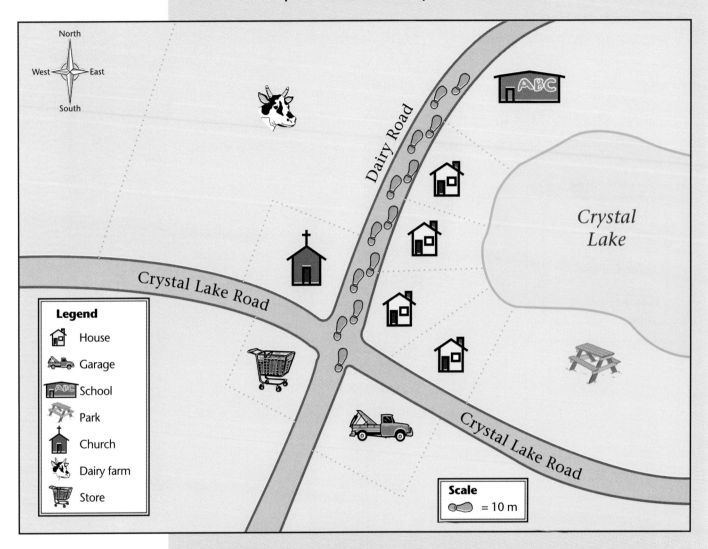

1. Find the compass rose. Is north toward the top or the bottom of the map?

2. What are the names of the two roads that go by the farm?

3. What colour is used to show water?

4. How many metres is it from the garage to the school?

Look again at these pictures and ideas from Chapter 3.
Then decide if you need to do more research to answer the
Big Question: *What kinds of services, utilities, and places do you
have in your community?*

▲ How do services help make our
communities healthy and safe?

▲ How do utilities make a
difference in our daily lives?

▲ What are some of the kinds of
places most communities have?

CHAPTER 4

GOVERNMENT

Imagine what your school would be like if no one was in charge! There would be nobody to make sure work got done, and nobody to help solve problems.

In your school, the principal and teachers are the leaders who make the rules and help solve problems. In your community, that job is done by a group of people called the **government**.

The Big Question for this chapter is: *What are the main responsibilities of community governments?* You can learn

- how people choose community leaders
- who is in the government
- what governments do

▲ At first, it might be fun to have no rules. But what kinds of problems might come up after a while?

Community Leaders

Preview to see what is in this section. Read the first few sentences under each heading. Look at the diagrams and photographs.

READING HINT

The governments of towns and cities are made up of the mayor and councillors. The mayor is the leader. The councillors are other people who work with the mayor to make decisions for the community.

People in towns and cities choose the mayor and councillors by voting in elections. There is an election every three years.

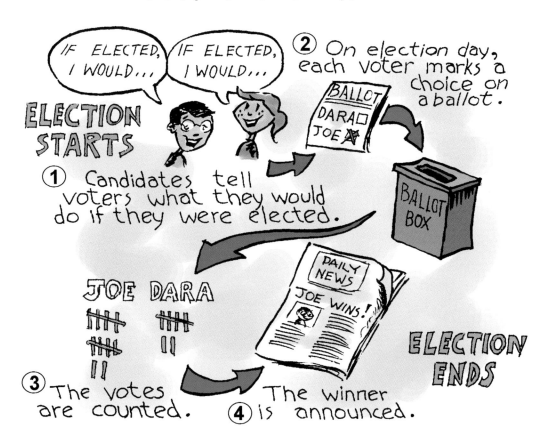

Working Together

After they are elected, the mayor and councillors make rules and decisions about how to keep the community a friendly and safe place to live.

When they have to make an important decision, the mayor and councillors start by collecting the information they need. Next, they discuss the pluses and minuses of different choices. Then they vote on what to do. It is the mayor's job to make sure everyone listens fairly to all the ideas.

Mayor Colin Kinsley

Colin Kinsley is the mayor of Prince George. Mayor Kinsley works with eight councillors to make decisions for the city.

This is the second time in a row that Colin Kinsley has been elected mayor. In the next election, people might pick a new mayor. What might make people vote for Colin Kinsley again? What might make them vote for a new mayor?

Aboriginal Communities

The leader in an Aboriginal community is called the chief. The chief can be an elected chief or a hereditary chief. A hereditary chief is the son or daughter, or niece or nephew, of the chief who had the job before.

Chiefs get help in making decisions from councillors and from the Elders. Councillors might be chosen in an election or appointed by the chief. The Elders are older people who know the traditions of the community. They have also had lots of practice solving problems.

Sometimes decisions are made by voting. Sometimes decisions are made after everyone talks things over and agrees on what to do.

Chief Marilyn Gabriel

Marilyn Gabriel is chief of the Kwantlen people. The Kwantlen are members of the Stó:lö [STO-loe] Nation. The people in her family have been leaders in the community for as long as anyone can remember. Marilyn Gabriel's father was the chief before her.

How do you think Chief Marilyn Gabriel learned how to be a responsible leader?

▲ Marilyn Gabriel (in the middle) and her councillors Les Antone and Tumia Gludo.

YOUR TURN

Make a diagram that shows how the government in your community is organized. You might have to do some research to find the information you need.

Here are two different kinds of diagrams you could make. Choose one kind for your diagram.

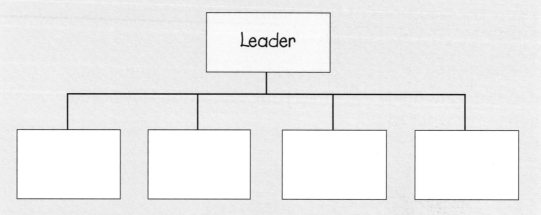

▲ In this kind of diagram, put the name of the leader in the top box. Then add one box for each councillor.

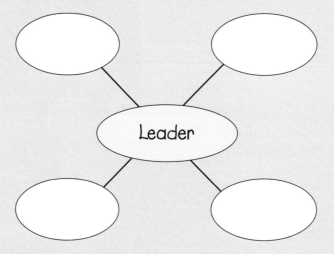

▲ In this kind of diagram, put the name of the leader in the middle circle. Then add one circle for each councillor.

Big Responsibilities

When you look at pictures, be sure to read the captions (the words with the pictures). Captions explain what the pictures show.

READING HINT

The main responsibility of a community government is to make sure people get the everyday and emergency services they need. The government also has to make plans for places where people can work, live, shop, and play.

This page and the next show some examples of government responsibilities. You can see that it is a big job!

The government makes ▶ regulations for utilities and services. A regulation is a rule everyone in the community must follow.

◀ The government decides how much money to spend on community centres, libraries, and recreation.

As the community grows, ▶
the government has to
make plans so that some
land is kept for parks.

▲ The government is responsible for street
lights, traffic lights, sidewalks, and
everything else that keeps roads safe.

▲ The government has
to make sure there is
enough money to buy
new emergency equipment
when it is needed.

YOUR TURN

Draw pictures that show some of the things the government
is responsible for in your community. You might know about
some projects that are important in your community right now.

Interview with a Councillor

In an interview, one person asks questions and another person answers. Look for the questions and answers in this interview.

READING HINT

Sharon Shepherd is a councillor for the city of Kelowna. In this interview, she tells you what it is like to be a councillor.

◄ Here is Sharon Shepherd with the mayor of Kelowna and the other councillors.

Question:
What do you think is the most important job for the mayor and councillors?

Answer:
That is a hard question to answer! I think everything the community government does is important. Maybe the most important job is to make the regulations for services and utilities such as clean water, police, and garbage collection. These regulations make sure the community is a healthy and safe place to live.

Question:

What is one problem you are working on right now?

Answer:

I'm part of a group that is trying to find ways to help people understand the problem of dirty air. We want people to get their cars fixed if they are causing pollution and to trade smoky stoves for new ones. We want them to think twice before they cut down trees.

Question:

What is the hardest part of your job?

Answer:

The hardest part is making sure I make decisions that are good for the community. When people vote for you, they trust you to do that. It is also hard to find time to answer all the letters, e-mails, and phone calls I get every day.

Question:

What part of your job is the most fun?

Answer:

It's fun that I get to do something different every day and learn about all the different parts of the community. I also like meeting people and helping them with problems they have.

YOUR TURN

1. Think about how Sharon Shepherd answered the questions in this interview. Would you vote for her to be part of your community government? Why or why not?

2. Brainstorm questions you would like to ask the councillors in your community. Think about what really matters to you.

Use Questions in Research

A list of questions can help you stay focused when you do research in the library or use a computer. You can also use questions to interview someone.

These three steps can help you ask the kinds of questions that will get the information you need.

1. Write down the topic. It might help to complete this sentence:
I am doing this research because I want to find out . . .

2. Brainstorm all the questions you can think of.

3. Choose three or four of your most interesting questions.
These are questions that
   • keep to the topic
   • cannot be answered with "yes" or "no"
   • are about important facts and ideas

When you interview ▶
someone, nod your
head to show that you
are listening. If you
don't understand, ask
for more information.

Look again at these pictures and ideas from Chapter 4.
Then decide how you would answer the Big Question:
What are the main responsibilities of community governments?

◄ What did you learn about how the government is chosen in your community?

What are some of the responsibilities the government has in a community? ▶

◄ What do you think it would be like to be part of your community government?

CHAPTER 5

HISTORY

History is everything that has happened before today. It is about the people, places, and events in the past.

History is a mystery! It is a mystery because we can't go back in time to collect information. Instead, we have to look for clues in the things we have from the past and in the stories people tell.

The Big Question for this chapter is: *What are some ways to collect and organize information about the past?* You can read about

- the sources of information we have for the past
- how to use time order to organize a history presentation

▲ These students are visiting an old building in the historic town of Barkerville, BC. What historic places can you visit near your community?

Records of the Past

READING HINT

Think like a detective when you read the questions in this section. Put the clues together and decide what answer makes the most sense.

Historians are people who study the past. They spend their time looking for clues about what happened long ago. They might look at old objects or photographs, read old newspapers, or listen to old songs or stories. These are all records of the past.

Here's your chance to be a historian! The next pages show records of the past for one old building in Victoria. Use these clues to figure out what the building was used for.

1. Photograph of the Building

This photograph shows the building about 50 years after it was built.

What are your first ideas about what the building might have been used for? What makes you think that?

2. The Excavation

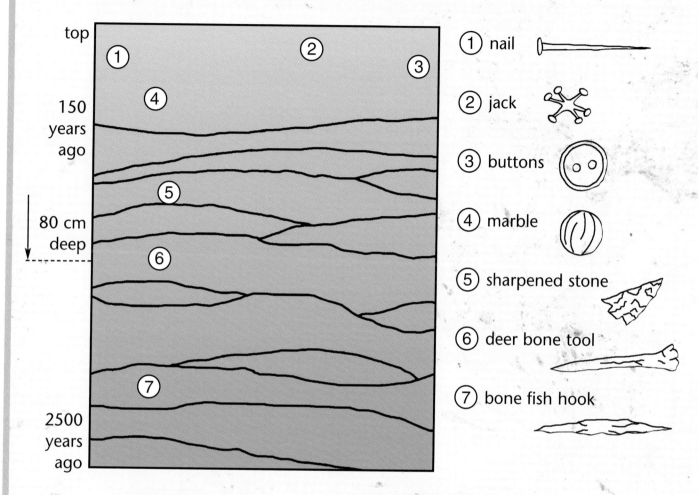

top

150 years ago

↓ 80 cm deep

2500 years ago

① nail

② jack

③ buttons

④ marble

⑤ sharpened stone

⑥ deer bone tool

⑦ bone fish hook

This diagram shows some of the things that researchers found when they dug a deep hole in the ground near the building.

Look at the things found during the excavation. Which things are clues that children used this building?

The sharpened stone was probably made by the people of the Kosapsom [ko-SAP-sum] Nation. What do you think it was used for?

3. Building Accounts

Date	Year: 1854 Item	Cost
August 30	J. Humphrey clearing land to begin work	0.8.4
September 1	2 pair oxen hauling timber	1.6.3
October 10	60 feet lumber	0.5.0
	75 lbs. nails	1.17.6
October 17	2 iron bars for chimney	0.10.0
October 18	5500 bricks	17.3.9
Date	Year: 1855 Item	Cost
February 23	200 feet of lumber for desks	1.12.4
February 27	12 hat pegs	0.6.0
March 2	large bell from the ship "Major Tompkins"	no cost
March 12	glass for windows	0.2.0
April 21	final payments	20.16.8

This is part of an old record that shows how much the building cost. The costs of the items are in pounds, shillings, and pence. This was the money people used at the time.

What other information do these building accounts give you? What do you think the bell was used for?

4. Photograph of Children

This photograph of the inside gives lots of clues about what the building was used for! What do you find most interesting?

YOUR TURN

1. Do some research to find a record of your past. You could look for a photograph or keepsake (something that is special to you). Adults who know about your past might be able to help.

2. Make a display or give a short talk to explain why the thing you have chosen is an important record of your past.

Telling History

READING HINT

"Donato's Life History" starts on this page and goes across to the next page. Plan how you will read the information on these pages.

Time Order

Time order is one way to organize a history presentation.

When you use time order, you start by describing the first thing that happened, then the next thing that happened, and so on to the end. Writing down the dates makes it clear.

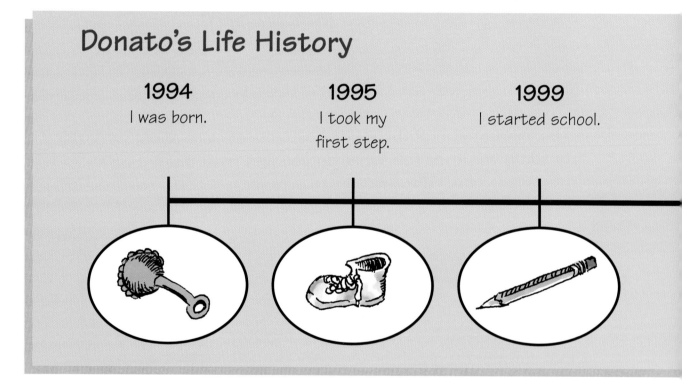

Donato's Life History

| 1994 | 1995 | 1999 |
| I was born. | I took my first step. | I started school. |

▲ The first thing to decide is when to start the history and when to end it. What would be the start and finish dates if this information was about you?

Key Events

Think how long it would take to describe everything that has happened to you since you were born. Even if you could, it would be too much information for anyone to read!

When historians write the history of a person or place, they choose the most important events. These are the key events. Key events are big changes or exciting things that happened.

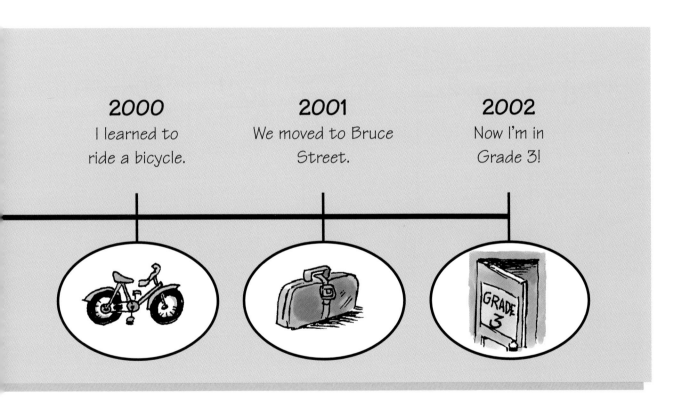

2000
I learned to ride a bicycle.

2001
We moved to Bruce Street.

2002
Now I'm in Grade 3!

YOUR TURN

Record the history of your life so far. Here's what to do.

1. Decide when to start and when to end.

2. Choose three or four key events for the middle. Pick important changes or exciting things that happened.

3. Record the date and some information about each key event. You might need to check some facts by talking to adults who know about your past.

4. Arrange your presentation in time order.

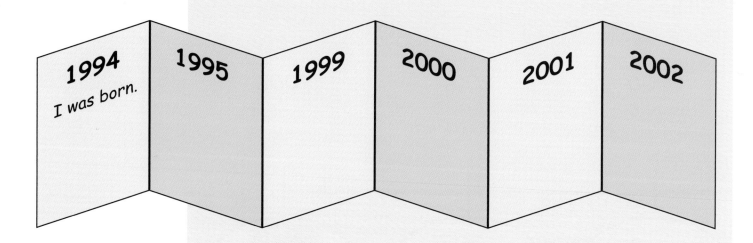

1994
I was born.

1995

1999

2000

2001

2002

▲ You could display your presentation like this.

Tell Fact from Fiction

When you collect information, you need to be able to tell the difference between fact and fiction. Here are some ways to tell the difference.

Fact
- The words and pictures give information about people, places, and things that are real.
- None of the information is made up by the writer.

> *Here is an example of fact:*
> At Horne Lake Caves Provincial Park on Vancouver Island, visitors can go into three long, winding caves.

Fiction
- The words and pictures tell a story about characters and their problems.
- The story might include some facts, but most of it is made up by the writer.

> *Here is an example of fiction:*
> Despina crawled along the slick, wet rock through the narrow part of the cave. Her flashlight flickered. "Oh, no," she thought. Suddenly, she was in total darkness.

Look again at these pictures and ideas from Chapter 5. Then decide how you would answer the Big Question: *What are some ways to collect and organize information about the past?*

Here is an example of fiction:
Despina crawled along the slick, wet rock thro⸱ part of the cave. Her flashlight flickered. "Oh, ⸱ Suddenly, she was in total darkness.

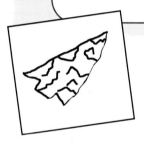

▲ What kind of information about the past interests you the most? What makes this kind of information interesting?

How can time order ▶ help you understand the past?

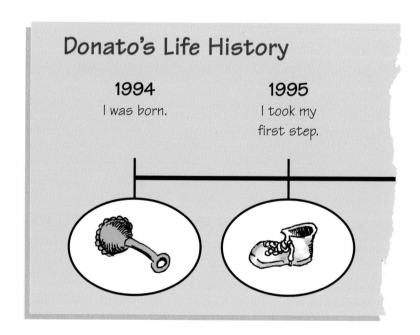

Donato's Life History

1994
I was born.

1995
I took my first step.

MAKING HISTORY

There are two things that are important in the history of almost all communities in British Columbia: **natural resources** and **transportation routes**.

Natural resources are things that the environment gives us, such as fish, trees, and soil.

A transportation route is a way to get from one place to another. In the past, trails and rivers were the main transportation routes. Today, we can travel on roads and railways and by boat and airplane.

The Big Question for this chapter is: *Why are natural resources and transportation routes so important to communities?* To help you answer this question, you can find out about

- British Columbia's natural resources
- how transportation routes help a community
- the histories of two communities in British Columbia

Natural Resources

READING HINT

Use the doughnut chart on this page to find out what natural resources you can read about in this section.

Natural resources are important because they give us what we need to live. Everything we eat, wear, or use is made from some kind of natural resource.

In many communities, natural resources are important in another way. They provide jobs for people. Some people work in jobs getting the resources. Other people work in jobs making the resources into products we can use.

British Columbia is rich in ▶ natural resources. This doughnut chart shows you the five main ones. You can read more about these resources on the next pages.

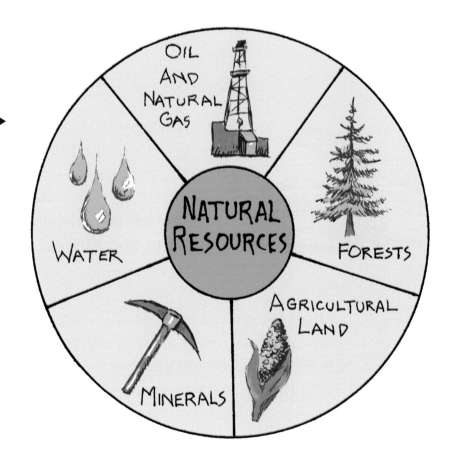

Forests

British Columbia has large areas of forest. Cutting down the trees is the first step in using this natural resource. This part of forestry is called logging.

The logs are sent to mills. In the mills, the logs are made into lumber, plywood, or paper. The wood or paper from a mill might go to a factory that makes other products. For example, wood is used to make furniture, and paper is used to make books.

Logging companies also plant young trees and care for them as they grow. These young trees will make new forests.

◀ Making products isn't the only use for forests. What does this picture show you about other ways forests are important?

Minerals

Minerals are found in rocks. Gold and copper are examples of minerals that are important natural resources. Workers use machines to dig through dirt and rock to find minerals. This is called mining.

Some minerals are sent to a kind of factory called a smelter. At a smelter, minerals are made into metals that we can use to make things such as nails and wire.

◄ When you drink from an aluminum pop can, you are using minerals. Aluminum is made from a mineral called bauxite. Before it goes to the smelter, bauxite looks like red dirt.

Coal
Coal is a special kind of mineral called a fossil fuel.

Fossil fuels come from plants and animals that died long ago. For millions of years, rocks pressed on the dead plants and animals. This turned them into rock, liquid, or gas. Fossil fuels contain a lot of energy. Coal burns when it is set on fire.

Oil and Natural Gas

Oil and natural gas are other forms of fossil fuels.

Oil is a thick liquid. To get oil, workers drill wells down to where the oil is lying between layers of rock.

Oil is pumped out of the ground and into pipes. The pipes take it to places where it is made into products we can use, such as gasoline and plastic.

Natural gas is trapped in spaces in the ground. Workers drill wells to get natural gas. The gas then travels in pipes to communities all over the province. Natural gas is used for heating and cooking.

How many things do you use that are made of plastic? How often do you ride in a vehicle that runs on gasoline?

DRILL

OIL

Agricultural Land

"Agriculture" is another word for farming and ranching.

There are many different kinds of farms. Some farmers grow fruit, vegetables, or wheat. Other farmers keep dairy cows for milk, or raise chickens or pigs. Ranchers usually raise cattle for beef.

Some crops that farmers grow, such as apples and lettuce, can be sold when they are fresh. Other crops are made into food products. For example, wheat is used to make bread and breakfast cereal.

Here's a lunch of ▶ milk and a chicken sandwich. Match each part of the meal to the plant or animal it came from.

CHAPTER 6

Water

Everyone needs water for drinking, cooking, and washing. We get fish and shellfish from rivers, lakes, and oceans. We also use water for play and sports.

It takes work and planning to care for water resources. We must keep our water clean and build pipes to carry the water to our communities. We also need to get rid of waste water in ways that are safe.

How can water also be used as a source of energy? Think about what you already know about electricity.

◀ There are two kinds of water resources: fresh water and salt (ocean) water. Which of these must be fresh water?

Pick one of British Columbia's natural resources. Make a doughnut chart that shows why the resource is important. Include some jobs people might have working with the resource.

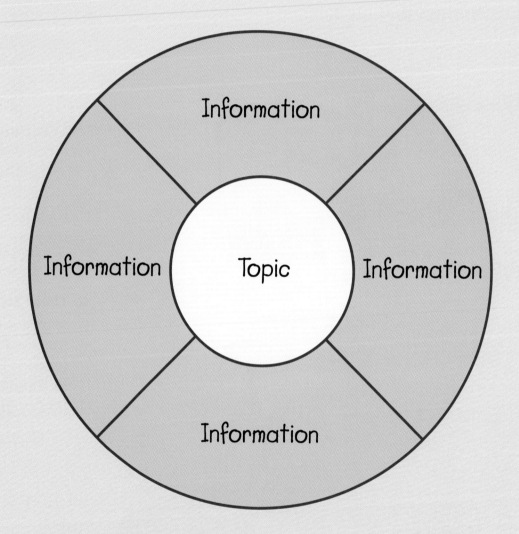

Information

Information

Topic

Information

Information

▲ In a doughnut chart, the topic goes in the middle and the information to explain it goes around the outside. The information can be in words or pictures.

Transportation Routes

Pause and think after each paragraph. Try saying the main idea in your own words.

READING HINT

Communities usually grow bigger if they are near transportation routes. People want to live close to transportation routes so they can get what they need to run their businesses.

Transportation routes make it easier for businesses to send their products to other places to sell. They also make it easier for people from other places to come to shop. More businesses mean more jobs, so more and more people come to the community.

A business is any place where people work to make money. A mill, a farm, and a store are all examples of businesses.

▲ Vancouver is the biggest community in British Columbia. Many businesses are here because the city has a large harbour where ships can dock.

YOUR TURN

Highways are important transportation routes in British Columbia. For each clue, use the map to find the name of the highway or community.

1. Take this highway to get from Prince George to Fort Nelson.

2. This community is at the south end of Highway 16 on the Queen Charlotte Islands.

3. Take this highway west from Prince George to get to Prince Rupert.

Comparing Communities

The reports in this section include bar graphs.
A bar graph can help you quickly see how much the
population has changed over time.

People choose locations for their communities that have useful
natural resources and are near good transportation routes.

Changes to the natural resources or transportation routes
can cause big changes in a community. These changes become
part of a community's history.

The reports in this section explain how natural resources
and transportation routes have been important in the history
of two BC communities: Ocean Falls and Chemainus.

Chemainus is in the
traditional lands of
the Chemainus First
Nation. Ocean Falls
is in the traditional
lands of the Heiltsuk
[HILE-tsuk] Nation.

Ocean Falls

Ocean Falls started as a community because of forestry. The location was especially good because there were lots of big trees to log. There was also water to provide electricity to run a sawmill that made lumber and a pulp mill that made paper.

The first mill was built in 1909. Many people came to Ocean Falls to work at the mill. The community soon had a population of 4000. There were no roads to the community. People had to come by boat. Later, people could fly into the town by plane.

Then . . .

▲ This shows the pulp mill and some houses in Ocean Falls in the 1920s. Notice the tall smokestack on the pulp mill.

Big Changes

By the 1970s, there were problems in Ocean Falls.

The trees near the community had all been cut down. It was hard to get to the other trees, and it cost a lot of money to cut them down. Also, the mill was old and needed repairs. People tried to keep the mill running, but they finally had to close it.

People liked their community, but there wasn't any work for them. There were still no roads into the town. Most people decided to move away to find new jobs. In 2001, only about 40 people lived in Ocean Falls.

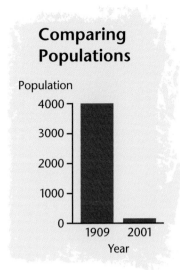

Comparing Populations

Now . . .

▲ Today, most of the buildings in Ocean Falls are empty. What else in this photograph shows the low population?

Chemainus

Chemainus grew as a community because of forestry and mining. The first sawmill was built in 1862. There was also a copper mine nearby.

Then . . .

▲ This photograph shows the Chemainus sawmill in the 1940s. What other parts of the community can you see?

Big Changes

After 100 years, there weren't many trees left in the area, and the copper was all gone. By 1983, the mine had closed, and the big sawmill had shut down. A new mill opened, but it didn't have jobs for as many people. The community was in trouble!

New Idea

Some people thought that Chemainus could be a good place for tourists to visit. It is located near the main highway on Vancouver Island, so many people drive past all year long.

People in the community decided to paint murals to tell the history of their town. They hoped tourists would stop to look at the murals.

People in the community opened gift shops and restaurants so there would be other things for visitors to do. They also built a theatre. Today, Chemainus is doing well because it is an interesting place to visit. About 300 000 tourists visit the town each year!

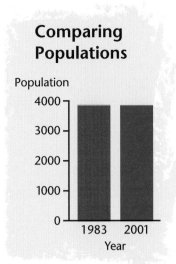

Comparing Populations

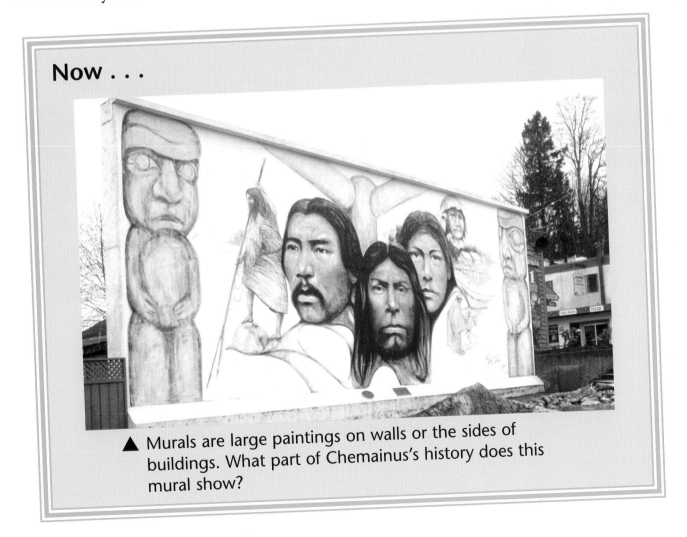

Now . . .

▲ Murals are large paintings on walls or the sides of buildings. What part of Chemainus's history does this mural show?

YOUR TURN

Use a Venn diagram to compare the histories of Chemainus and Ocean Falls.

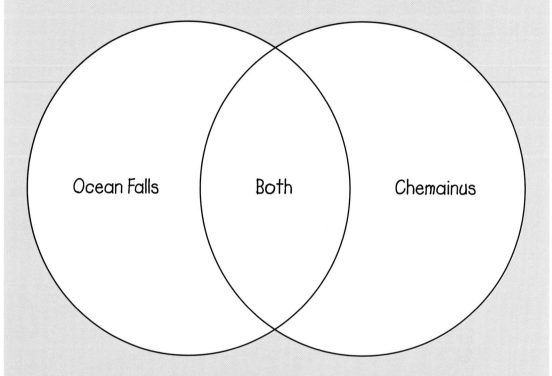

Ocean Falls   Both   Chemainus

▲ In a Venn diagram, you put the things that are the same in the middle and the things that are different on the sides.

Find Information in Pictures

Photographs and drawings are important sources of information.

Here are some questions to ask yourself when you look at a photograph or drawing:

- What do I notice first?
- What is the main idea in this drawing or photograph?
- What other details can I see?

Main idea: Large ships and water tell you that this photograph shows a big harbour.

Detail: The number of buildings shows that this is a big city.

Detail: Lumber is shipped from this harbour.

Look again at these pictures and ideas from Chapter 6. Then decide how you would answer the Big Question: *Why are natural resources and transportation routes so important to communities?*

What are two reasons why ▶ people would want to live in a place that has lots of natural resources?

▲ What is one main idea you learned about how transportation routes make a difference in a community's history?

CHAPTER 7

HERITAGE

Your **heritage** is everything that has come to you from the past. This includes your **culture** — the ideas and ways of doing things that are important in your family.

Like you, British Columbia also has a heritage. It includes the cultures of everyone who has lived in the province during its history. That adds up to a lot of different cultures!

The Big Question for this chapter is: *What are some of the cultures that make up British Columbia's heritage?* You can read information on
- the parts that make up culture
- celebrations in different cultures

When we work and ▶
play together, we
can learn about each
other's cultures.
What cultures do you
know about in your
community?

Culture

READING HINT

If you need a reminder of what traditions are, look in the glossary on pages 150–151.

Before you research cultures in British Columbia, you need to know something about the parts of culture.

Culture is the way we live our lives. It includes everyday things, such as what we eat or what we wear. It also includes special things, such as celebrations and traditions. This web shows you some of the parts of culture.

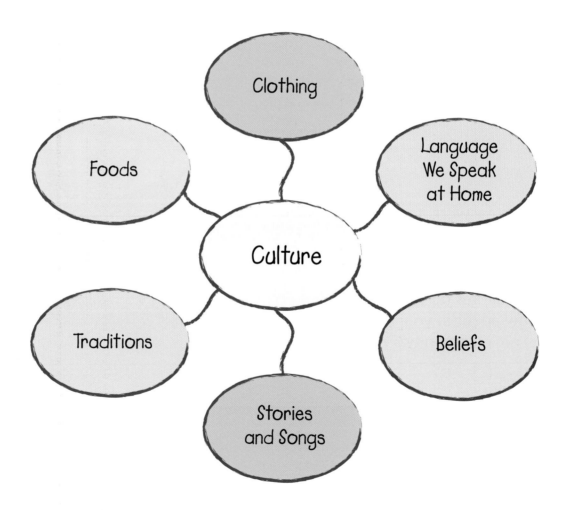

Diversity

Diversity means "interesting differences." Diversity is what you will find when you research cultures.

Here are breakfasts from different cultures. What is the same about these breakfasts? What is different? What do you have for breakfast?

Cold Rice and Fish

Bread and Coffee

Cereal and Milk

Beans and Tortillas

YOUR TURN

Make a web that shows some of the parts of your culture. Think about your everyday life and about things that are special in your family.

Celebrating

READING HINT

Think about how the celebrations described in this section are like celebrations in your life.

Here are some photographs and keepsakes from celebrations in BC communities. Looking at these can help you understand the diversity that makes up British Columbia's heritage.

Diwali

Every October or November, people of Indian heritage celebrate Diwali [dee-WAHL-ee]. This is a time to wish friends good luck and wealth. It is a tradition to light rows of candles or small oil lamps called diyas [DEE-yahs] and set off fireworks. People get together with family and friends. They might exchange small gifts such as fruit and nuts.

Oktoberfest

In October, people of German heritage have large parties where everyone comes together to play music, dance, eat, and drink. This is a tradition that started long ago to celebrate a royal wedding.

Chinese New Year

People of Chinese heritage celebrate their new year in late January or early February. In China, this celebration is a quiet family event. In other parts of the world, it includes noisy parades with people dancing as lions and dragons.

Scottish Dancing

Many people of Scottish heritage enjoy traditional Scottish dancing. Young people often perform at community events.

Heritage Fact

British Columbia is part of the country of Canada. French and English are Canada's two official languages. In the province of Québec, most people speak French, and French traditions are very important.

Festival du Bois

Many people in the community of Maillardville, BC, are of French-Canadian heritage. At the Festival du Bois [FES-tih-val du BWAH], the community invites others to join in for traditional French-Canadian music, food, and entertainment.

Hanukkah

People of Jewish heritage celebrate Hanukkah [HAH-nah-kuh] in December. Families light candles in memory of an important event in Jewish history. Children play special games while the candles are lit, and everyone enjoys traditional foods.

Heritage Fact

In the early part of Canada's history, many French men married Aboriginal women. Métis culture came from these marriages. The culture is a mix of Aboriginal and French traditions.

Métis Hoe-Down

Many communities in British Columbia hold Métis [may-TEE] celebrations during the year. In Chilliwack, this includes setting up a traditional buffalo-hunting camp with teepees flying the Métis flag.

Multicultural Festivals

"Multiculture" means "many cultures." In a multicultural festival, people from a variety of cultures share music, dance, and food. Many communities have these kinds of celebrations.

YOUR TURN

Give an oral report on a celebration, a special food, or a tradition that interests you. Your topic might be something important to you and your family. Or you might choose something interesting from another culture.

Give an Oral Presentation

Here are some hints for organizing an oral presentation.

- Begin by telling what your topic is.
- Pick two or three main ideas to explain.
- Put the facts and ideas in an order that makes sense.
- Make the ending strong so that it is clear you are finished.

▲ When you give your presentation, speak loudly enough for everyone to hear. Speak slowly enough to give people time to think about what you are saying.

Look again at these pictures and ideas from Chapter 7. Then decide how you would answer the Big Question: *What are some of the cultures that make up British Columbia's heritage?*

▲ What does diversity mean?

◀ What other cultures do you know about that are not shown in this textbook?

CHAPTER 8

VANDERHOOF

This whole chapter is a report on the history of one community in British Columbia. The community is Vanderhoof.

The report includes information on the natural resources and transportation routes that helped the community grow. It also tells you about some of the cultures that make up the community's heritage.

The Big Question for this chapter is: *How can reading this report help you do your own report on the history of a community?* You can think about

- topics to include
- questions to ask
- how to organize the information

▲ You might be able to find information on the history of your community in books. What other sources of information can you think of for a community history?

A History of Vanderhoof

READING HINT

Notice how time order has been used to organize this report.

Population

In 2001, Vanderhoof's population was 4400. Another 14 000 people lived near the town on farms and ranches.

Location

Vanderhoof is beside the Nechako River, exactly in the middle of British Columbia. The Nechako River is in the traditional lands of the Dakelh [da-KEL]. The Saik'uz [sigh-k'UZ] are the Dakelh people with lands closest to Vanderhoof.

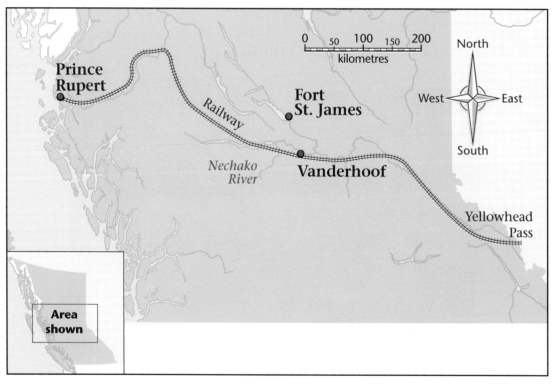

▲ This map shows the three communities you need to know about to understand the history of Vanderhoof. What else is shown on the map? Why do you think this might be important?

Environment

The Nechako River is in the Interior Plateau region of British Columbia. The land is quite flat, with mountains in the distance.

This area has many small rivers and lakes. There are some grasslands but also large areas of forest. The forests are a mix of pine, spruce, fir, balsam, and poplar trees.

Winters are long and cold. Summers are dry and warm.

Evergreen trees are ▶ good for making lumber or paper.

◀ The flat land around Vanderhoof makes the area good for growing hay, grain, and other feed for farm animals.

The First People

The Saik'uz were the first people to live in the Vanderhoof area. The traditional name for the area is Kelcucheck. This means "river mouth." It is a good name because this is where a smaller river joins the Nechako.

The Saik'uz used the river and forest resources for food, shelter, and clothing. They travelled the rivers by canoe. In spring and summer, large groups of people gathered by the rivers to catch salmon. People also hunted and trapped forest animals such as deer and black bears.

▲ This painting by Saik'uz artist Shana Schwentner shows a fishing camp long ago. Where do you think she got the information to do this art and the art on the next page?

1806: Newcomers

In 1806, a man called Simon Fraser came to the Nechako River area. He was a fur trader of Scottish heritage. He hoped the Dakelh could help him get the furs of animals such as beaver and fox.

Simon Fraser set up a trading fort. Dakelh hunters brought furs to the fort to trade for things such as guns and pots.

Each year, more fur traders arrived. People also came to look for gold. The fort became a small community called Fort St. James.

Heritage!

The fur traders were men of Métis, French, English, and Scottish heritage. Traders travelled in groups.

▲ Simon Fraser hired Aboriginal guides for his trips. Why would the Saik'uz and their neighbours be good guides for the forests and rivers near Vanderhoof?

1914: The Railway

In 1914, the Grand Trunk Pacific Railway company built a railway all the way from Winnipeg, Manitoba, to Prince Rupert, BC.

The railway didn't go to Fort St. James because it was better to build the tracks closer to the Nechako River. That way, boats could bring the supplies that the workers needed.

The railway made it easier for **settlers** to move to the area. Settlers were newcomers who wanted to start farms or ranches. The government of British Columbia made the Saik'uz and other Aboriginal peoples move onto reserves so that the settlers could have the land.

Heritage!

Many early settlers were Mennonites who came from Russia and Germany. They were good farmers.

▲ This shows a group of Mennonite settlers arriving in Vanderhoof in 1918. How did they travel?

1920s: The Village of Vanderhoof

The company that built the railway wanted more people to settle near the rail line, so they hired a man named Herbert Vanderhoof to help build a community.

Herbert Vanderhoof made a plan for the community. Then he spread the news around that people could buy good farmland in the area for a very cheap price. Many people came to start farming. By 1926, there were enough people to form the village of Vanderhoof.

Heritage!

Many men came from China to work on building the new railways in Canada. The O.K. Café was started by two men of Chinese heritage: Tim Chow and George Cheuy.

◄ The O.K. Café opened in 1920. You can still eat here! In the early days, there was no electricity or running water. How do you think people got water and light?

1950s: Forestry and Electricity

Vanderhoof really started to grow in the 1950s. People came to the area because there were lots of jobs in forestry. British Columbia's communities were growing quickly, and everybody needed lumber for building.

See page 29 for a reminder of how hydroelectric dams work.

In 1952, nearly 1500 people came to the area to work on building the Kenney Dam. This dam was being built to send water to a hydroelectric station near the coast. After the dam was built, many of the workers stayed in the area to work in forestry or agriculture.

This shows men ▶ moving logs into the water in 1950. How do you think logging has changed since then?

CHAPTER 8

Vanderhoof Today

Between the 1950s and today, Vanderhoof's population has grown a little, but not a lot.

Forestry and agriculture are still the most important kinds of work. Tourism is also important. Visitors like to come to the rivers, lakes, and forests for their holidays.

This shows the ▶ main highway into Vanderhoof. What can you tell about the community from this photograph?

◀ This is a photograph of the Stoney Creek Multiplex. It is a recreation centre built by the Saik'uz. It is used for sports and community events.

YOUR TURN

Choose one part of Vanderhoof's history and show it in a storyboard. You could choose one of these parts of Vanderhoof's history:

- Saik'uz life and Simon Fraser
- the big changes that happened from 1914 to 1926
- the history from 1950 to today

My Storyboard

1. I was born (1994)

2. I took my first step (1995)

3. I started school (1999)

▲ In a storyboard, you make pictures of key events and arrange them in time order. You can include captions to explain the pictures. This shows how a storyboard of a person's life might start out.

Look again at these pictures and ideas from Chapter 8.
Then decide how you would answer the Big Question:
How can reading this report help you do your own report on the history of a community?

Heritage!

Many early settlers were Mennonites who came from Russia and Germany. They were good farmers.

▲ What three questions would you ask if you were doing a community history?

How can time order ▶ help you clearly show the history of a place?

1806: Newcomers

1914: The Railway

1920s: The Village of Vanderhoof

CHAPTER 9

OUR LAND

British Columbia is one province in the country of Canada.

Canada is made up of ten provinces and three territories. It is so big that it can take ten days to drive from one side to the other. If you stopped to look at all the different parts of the country, it would take much longer.

The Big Question for this chapter is: *What are the main physical features of the provinces and territories of Canada?* You can

- look at some maps of Canada
- find out about some of the sites to see in Canada

◄ One way to learn about Canada is to travel and see it for yourself. This family is visiting a lighthouse in the province of Nova Scotia. What are other ways you could find information about your country?

Canada in Maps

This section has two maps of Canada. Notice what is on the second map that is not on the first one.

READING HINT

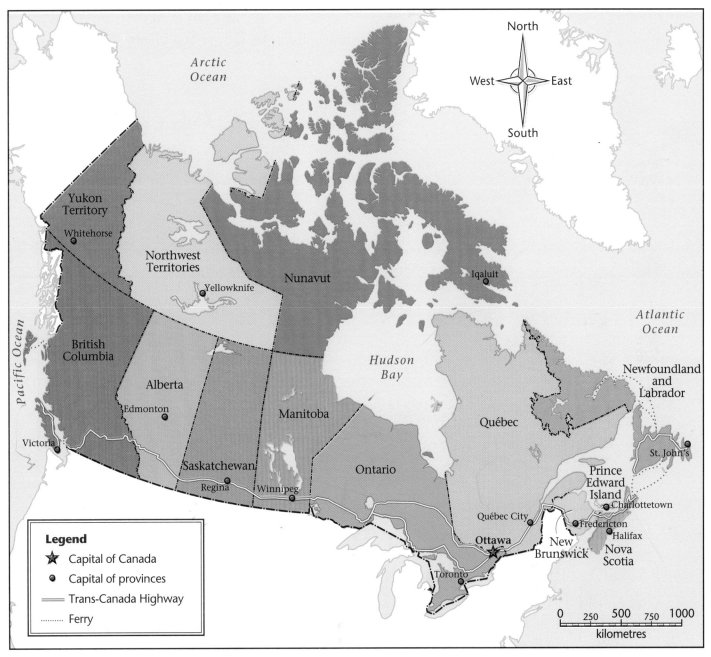

North

West • East

South

Arctic Ocean

Yukon Territory

• Whitehorse

Northwest Territories

• Yellowknife

Nunavut

• Iqaluit

Pacific Ocean

British Columbia

Alberta

• Edmonton

Victoria •

Saskatchewan

Regina •

Winnipeg •

Manitoba

Hudson Bay

Ontario

Atlantic Ocean

Newfoundland and Labrador

St. John's •

Québec

Québec City •

Ottawa ☆

Toronto •

New Brunswick

Fredericton •

Prince Edward Island

Charlottetown •

Halifax •

Nova Scotia

Legend

☆ Capital of Canada

• Capital of provinces

— Trans-Canada Highway

...... Ferry

0   250   500   750   1000

kilometres

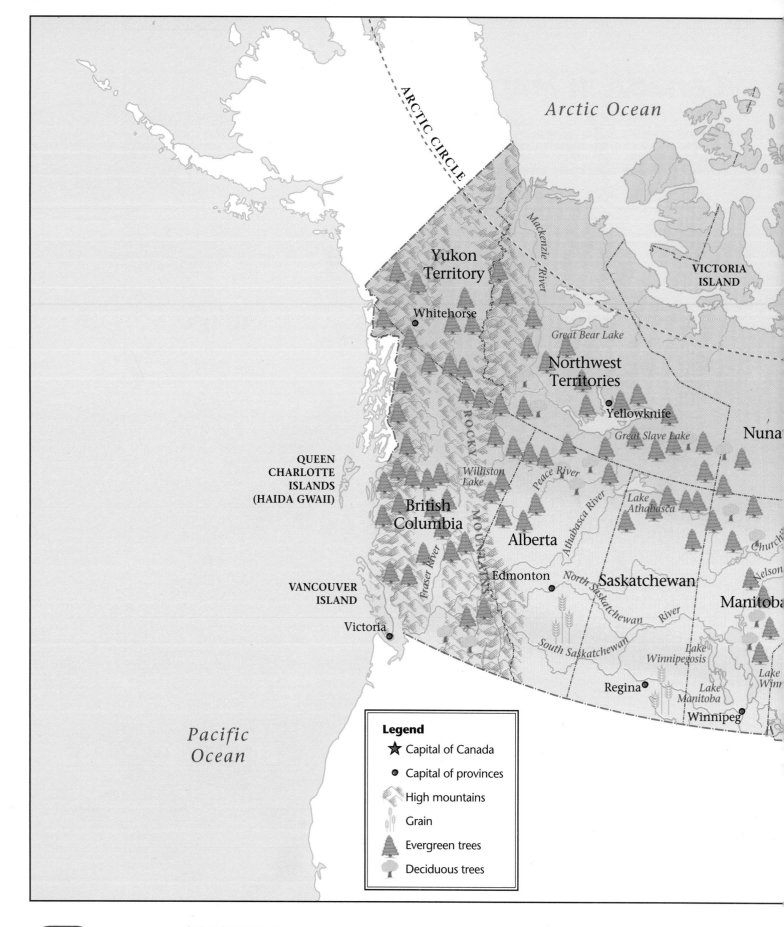

Legend
★ Capital of Canada
● Capital of provinces
High mountains
Grain
Evergreen trees
Deciduous trees

North
West · East
South

BAFFIN ISLAND

ARCTIC CIRCLE

Iqaluit

Hudson Bay

Newfoundland and Labrador

Smallwood Reservoir

St. John's

Canadian Weather
Canada is famous for its long, cold winters. Many areas get a lot of snow. The weather is warmest in the southern part of the country. It gets colder as you go north. In the south, summers can be hot. In the north, they are cooler.

Ontario

Québec

Québec City

St. Lawrence River

Prince Edward Island

New Brunswick

CAPE BRETON ISLAND

Charlottetown

Fredericton

Halifax

Atlantic Ocean

Nova Scotia

Great Lakes

Superior

Ottawa

Lake Michigan

Lake Huron

Toronto

Lake Ontario

Lake Erie

0 125 250 375 500
kilometres

SMERE
AND

YOUR TURN

Make up questions for a Canada Quiz. Here are categories of questions you could include:

- names of provinces and territories
- capitals of provinces and territories
- lakes
- rivers
- mountains
- islands

Here are sample questions to give you some ideas.

Q Name a province that begins and ends with the letter "a."

A Alberta

Q In what territory is Great Bear Lake?

A Northwest Territories

Q Which is further north, Baffin Island or Vancouver Island?

A Baffin Island

Exploring Canada

There is a question with each photograph in this section. The written information can help you answer the question.

READING HINT

If you want to learn about the provinces and territories of Canada, you've got a lot of ground to cover! It's easier if you divide the country into regions.

A region of Canada is a group of provinces or territories that have some of the same environments and physical features. The map on this page shows you the regions of Canada. The rest of this section gives you more information about each region.

Canada's motto is "From sea to sea." Why is this a good choice?

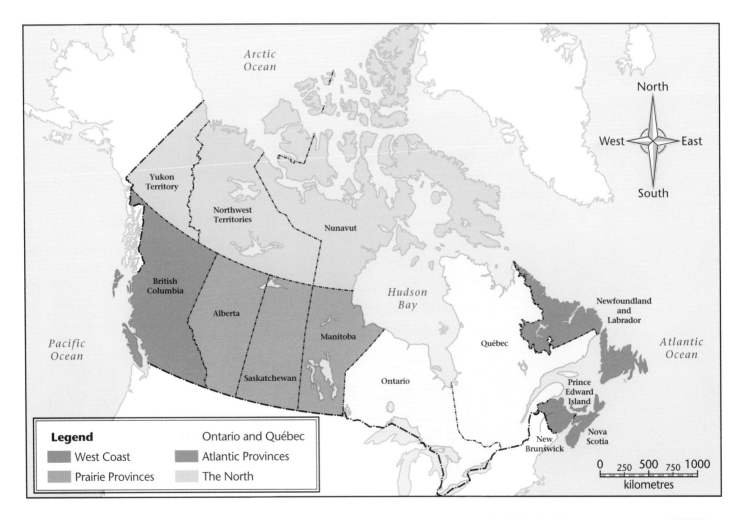

Legend
West Coast
Prairie Provinces
Ontario and Québec
Atlantic Provinces
The North

The West Coast

The West Coast region is made up of one province—British Columbia. You might already know something about BC's physical features. But there is always something more to learn.

Compared to other regions of Canada, British Columbia has many mountains. On the plateaus between the mountains and on the coast, there are some special environments, such as rain forests and deserts.

Coast Mountains

The Coast Mountains aren't as famous as the Rocky Mountains, but some of the mountains are higher than the ones in the Rockies.

▲ High mountains often have patches of snow even in the summer. Why do you think this is so?

Rain Forest

The coast of British Columbia does not get as cold or as hot as the rest of Canada. Very little snow falls on the coast, but it rains a lot. This weather is perfect for rain forests. Rain forests are thick forests of large evergreen trees. Many of the trees are hundreds of years old.

Fun Fact
Henderson Lake on Vancouver Island is the rainiest spot in Canada. In 1997, it got a record 8997 mm of rain!

▲ What word would you use to describe the tree trunks in this photograph?

Desert

Canada's only hot desert is near the community of Osoyoos [uh-SOY-us]. This is a small area, but there are some plants and animals here that you can't find in any other part of the country.

◀ What are the signs that tell you this is a desert?

The Prairie Provinces

The southern parts of Alberta, Saskatchewan, and Manitoba are prairie. Prairie is flat land with rich soil. It makes good farmland. The Prairie Provinces have some of the largest farms and cattle ranches in the world.

As you go north, there are large areas of forest. In fact, there are more forests than prairies in the Prairie Provinces!

Alberta Foothills

The border between British Columbia and Alberta goes along the Rocky Mountains. As you go east into Alberta, the mountains get smaller and rounder. These are called foothills. There are large cattle ranches in the foothills.

▲ This photograph shows cattle grazing in the Alberta foothills. What mountains can you see in the background?

Saskatchewan Wheat Farms

The most important crop in Saskatchewan is wheat. Wheat is a kind of grain. The seeds are ground to make flour. Most of the wheat used in Canada comes from Saskatchewan.

Fun Fact
The sunniest place in Canada is Estevan, Saskatchewan. It gets about 2540 hours of sunshine a year.

▲ What do you eat that is made from wheat?

Manitoba Forests

The forests in Manitoba are a mix of different kinds of trees. Some trees are evergreens. Others are deciduous. Deciduous trees have leaves that turn colour and fall off in the autumn.

◄ What time of year does this photograph of Manitoba forests show?

Ontario and Québec

The provinces of Ontario and Québec make up a region of their own. This region has the largest population of all the regions. It includes Ottawa. Ottawa is the capital of Canada.

The south has large areas of rich soil that is good for farming. There are also thick forests. As you go north, the forests get thinner. There are also areas of soft, wet land called muskeg. You can find these same types of environments in the north of other provinces.

Niagara Falls

Niagara Falls in Ontario is one of the world's most famous waterfalls. Huge amounts of water drop 100 metres between Lake Ontario and Lake Erie.

What do you think it ▶ sounds like when you are standing near the falls?

Northern Ontario Moose

There are thousands of small rivers and ponds in northern Ontario and Québec. This is the perfect home for moose. They eat plants that grow at the edge of the water.

◀ What do you think this moose cow and her calves are doing here at the edge of the water?

St. Lawrence River

The St. Lawrence River is an important transportation route between the Atlantic Ocean and the provinces of Québec and Ontario. There are many farms beside the river because the soil is so rich.

◀ This shows the St. Lawrence River near Québec City. The three largest cities in Québec are on the St. Lawrence River. Why might that be?

The Atlantic Provinces

The Atlantic Provinces include New Brunswick, Nova Scotia, Newfoundland and Labrador, and Prince Edward Island. This region is located near the Atlantic Ocean. Prince Edward Island and Newfoundland are islands, so they are actually in the ocean.

Fish and other seafood are important resources in this region. There are also forests and farmland.

The Bay of Fundy

The Bay of Fundy is between New Brunswick and Nova Scotia. It has the highest tides in the world. At high tide, the water rises 16 metres.

▲ What will happen to the boats when the tide comes in?

Coast of Newfoundland

The coast of Newfoundland is rocky and steep. In winter, strong winds send the ocean waves crashing onto the shore.

▲ Why do you think this community is built on a bay instead of on the shore that is open to the ocean?

Prince Edward Island Farms

Many different fruits and vegetables are grown on farms in the Atlantic Provinces. Prince Edward Island is famous for its potatoes.

◀ What do you notice about the colour of the soil on this Prince Edward Island farm?

—Treeline

The North

The North is famous for cold weather. Summer is cool and only about two months long. In winter, it can get very cold and windy. Parts of the North are so dry that they are deserts.

The physical features in this large area include mountains, plateaus, and low hills. There are many lakes and rivers.

Tundra

North of the treeline, it is too cold for forests. Different kinds of grasses and small plants called lichens [LYE-kuns] grow in the region, but only a few bushes and small trees. This kind of environment is called tundra.

▲ This photograph shows caribou grazing on the tundra in the Northwest Territories. What kinds of plants could they eat?

Yukon Territory

Most of Yukon Territory is south of the treeline. The land is rugged, and there are few roads. Transportation can be difficult, especially in winter when snow blocks the roads and railway tracks.

Fun Fact
The highest mountain in Canada is Mt. Logan in Yukon Territory. The longest river in Canada is the Mackenzie River in the Northwest Territories.

▲ This is the White Pass and Yukon Railway. What do you think the red part on the front of the engine is for?

Ellesmere Island

Much of the territory of Nunavut [NOON-ah-voot] is made up of islands. A group of islands like this is called an archipelago [ar-kuh-PEL-ah-go]. This group of islands is the largest archipelago in the world. It includes Ellesmere Island. Ellesmere Island is the northern-most island in Canada.

◀ These walrus are resting on ice near Ellesmere Island. Why do you think it gets so cold here?

YOUR TURN

Imagine you have been hired to make a video about the physical features of Canada.

1. Use a map of Canada to help you plan your route and decide which places to visit. You can go anywhere you want, as long as you go to at least one province or territory in each region.

2. Make a storyboard that describes what you would show people about each place. If you need a reminder about storyboards, see page 98.

Do Some Research!
Your textbook only has a little information about each region of Canada. You might have some questions.

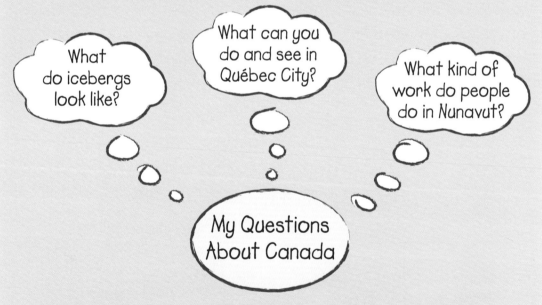

You could look for information at the library or at a Web site. You could also e-mail students in other parts of the country and ask them about the interesting physical features near their communities.

E-mail

E-mail is mail that you send and receive with a computer. Here's how to make friends and stay safe when you're e-mailing.

Be Polite!

Be as polite when you are writing an e-mail as you would be if you were talking to the person.

Stay Safe!

You never know for sure who is reading your e-mail or who is sending you a message. Here are some tips for staying safe:

- Never give your full name, address, or phone number.
- Don't tell where you play or go to school.
- Never make plans to meet an e-mail buddy without talking it over with an adult you know and trust.
- If a message bothers you or doesn't seem right, show it to an adult.

> **Some special symbols you can use:**
>
> :-) (happy — or "This is a joke")
>
> :-((sad)
>
> :-o (surprised)

The Big Question for this chapter is: *What are the main physical features of the provinces and territories of Canada?*

How could you show what you've learned about the physical features of Canada? You might think of some ways if you look again at these pictures and ideas from Chapter 9.

Fun Fact
Henderson Lake on Vancouver Island is the rainiest spot in Canada. In 1997, it got a record 8997 mm of rain!

CHAPTER 10

O CANADA!

If you travelled across Canada, you would meet Canadians from many different cultures.

In all provinces and territories of Canada, you can find the same diversity that you can find in communities in British Columbia. This diversity doesn't stop us from sharing some important ideas, though!

The Big Question for this chapter is: *What are some of the important ideas and symbols that are special to Canada?* You can read information on

- Canadian ideas about rights and responsibilities
- Canada's symbols
- what it means to be a Canadian citizen

◀ July 1 is Canada Day. That's when we celebrate everything that is special about Canada. How can you tell this is a Canada Day celebration?

Important Ideas

READING HINT

This section is about rights and responsibilities. Before you read, think of other times you have talked about this topic in your class.

One of the special things about Canada is that we have laws to help make sure the whole country is a friendly and safe place to live.

In your class or school, you may have a list of rights and responsibilities for people to follow. These rules help everyone get along.

Canada has something like a list of rights and responsibilities for the whole country. It is called the *Canadian Charter of Rights and Freedoms*. The Charter is a set of laws that people who live in Canada or who visit Canada must follow.

▲ The Royal Canadian Mounted Police (RCMP) help make sure that people in Canada obey the laws. This RCMP member is in front of the Parliament Buildings in Ottawa. This is where Canada's laws are made.

What the Charter Says

There are many parts to the *Canadian Charter of Rights and Freedoms*. Here is the main idea.

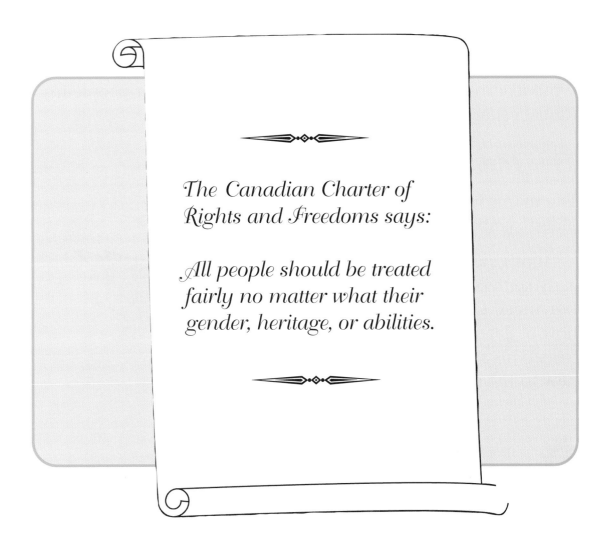

The Canadian Charter of Rights and Freedoms says:

All people should be treated fairly no matter what their gender, heritage, or abilities.

YOUR TURN

The Charter tells you what your rights are when you are in Canada. Make your own charter of matching responsibilities.

Symbols of Canada

READING HINT

In this section, the sidebars help you think about what you are reading. On each page, read the information first and then read the sidebar.

Canada's symbols are part of our Canadian traditions. These symbols can remind us of the ideas and history that people in Canada share.

The Maple Leaf

The maple leaf is one of Canada's oldest symbols.

Canadians often send maple syrup to friends in other parts of the world. What makes maple syrup a good choice?

Aboriginal peoples showed early settlers in the Atlantic Provinces, Ontario, and Québec how to get sap from sugar maple trees. This sweet treat was something new to the settlers.

When important people from England visited, settlers wore real maple leaves as a symbol of their new home. That was about 200 years ago!

The Canadian Flag

Canada used to have another flag. It included symbols that showed Canada's British heritage.

In 1964, Canada was only three years away from its 100th birthday. The government of Canada decided that the country needed a new flag to celebrate. It invited Canadians to send in their ideas for what to show on the flag.

Members of the government voted to choose one design. On 15 February 1965, Canada's new flag was raised for the first time.

Some people wanted the bars on the side of the flag to be blue. What could that be a symbol of?

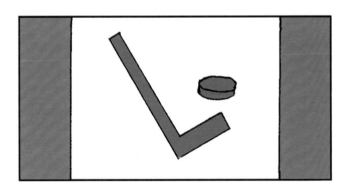

▲ Here is one person's idea for a Canadian flag. What does it show? Why might someone think this was a good symbol for Canada?

The Beaver

Early in Canada's history, many people in other parts of the world wanted hats made of beaver fur. One of the main reasons newcomers came to Canada was to get beaver furs.

If there had been no beavers in Canada, there might not have been a fur trade. The fur trade is an important part of Canada's history.

Which Canadian coin has a beaver on it?

YOUR TURN

The maple leaf, the flag, and the beaver are three of Canada's official symbols. That means they are ones that the government uses.

Make your own symbol for Canada. Explain what your symbol shows and why it is important to Canada.

A Canadian Citizen

When you read the "Welcome!" part of this section, think about a time you went to a new place. How did it feel?

READING HINT

A **Canadian citizen** is a person whose main home is in Canada. You can live in Canada if you are not a citizen. But being a citizen gives you special rights, such as the right to vote for the leaders of the country.

Becoming Canadian

Some people are Canadian citizens because they were born in Canada or because one of their parents is Canadian.

Other people become Canadian citizens by learning about Canada and taking an oath to follow the laws of the country. Taking an oath is like making a very important promise.

◀ This is a special day! These people are becoming Canadians. How do you think they feel?

O CANADA!

Welcome!

To help new Canadian citizens feel welcome, students from all across Canada took part in the Welcome Home Campaign. They wrote letters and poems and drew pictures to give to new Canadians.

Here are examples of their work. Notice the Canadian symbols and the important ideas about Canada these students included.

W e are

E xcited to have you

L ive here in

C anada!

O n this day

M ake Canada your home.

E njoy!!

From Camille

Dear Newcomer:

We would like to welcome you to our great country that is full of freedom and peace. We hope you enjoy it as much as we do.

We know how hard it must have been to come to a new country. We understand this and we hope that it was all worth it in the end.

We would like to say Congratulations and Welcome Home.

From Amie and Natasha

YOUR TURN

Write your own letter or poem or draw your own picture to welcome new Canadian citizens. Make sure you tell or show them something about Canada.

Look again at these pictures and ideas from Chapter 10. Then decide how you would answer the Big Question: *What are some of the important ideas and symbols that are special to Canada?*

◀ What important idea about getting along with others is part of Canada's laws?

How do Canadian symbols ▶ help us feel that we are all part of one country?

CHAPTER 11

MONEY

Canadians are connected in many ways. We are connected by the land we live in, by important laws and ideas, and by our heritage. We are also connected by money!

No matter where we live in Canada, we all use the same kind of money. Other countries have their own money, so our money is special to Canada.

We use money to buy things. The Big Question for this chapter is: *What do we need to know to use money wisely?* You can read information about
- what Canadian money looks like
- what budgeting is
- how advertising tries to get you to buy things

The Royal Canadian Mint ▶ has places where money is made in Winnipeg and Ottawa. What do you think the man is pouring into the top of the machine?

Canadian Money

READING HINT

Look carefully at the examples of money on these two pages. Notice what has changed and what has stayed the same in how our money looks.

To use money wisely, you need to know what it looks like and what the different coins and bills are worth.

Dollars and Cents

You probably know that Canadian money is made up of dollars and cents. One dollar equals 100 cents. Another name for a $1.00 coin is a loonie.

Most things we buy cost more than $1.00. Counting out loonies and pennies takes a lot of time. To make it easier, we have coins and paper money in different amounts.

Designs for Money

The government of Canada decides what our money looks like. Sometimes the government changes the design, but our money always includes symbols of Canada. It sometimes includes pictures of famous people.

Here are some money designs from the past.

YOUR TURN

1. With a partner, talk about the money on these two pages. What Canadian symbols or famous person do you see? Does any of this money look like the money you have seen? If not, what is different?

2. Make your own design for Canadian money. Remember to use some Canadian symbols. You might want to include people who are famous in your school or community.

Budgeting

READING HINT

This section includes a cartoon. Look for details in the pictures. Notice how the artist shows what people are thinking.

Budgeting is figuring out what things cost and deciding what you can afford to buy.

To use money wisely, you need to think about what you want to spend your money on. You might also want to give money to a charity or save some for another day.

This cartoon shows you what Mark did with the $10.00 he got for his birthday. See if you agree with Mark's choices!

YOUR TURN

1. With a partner, talk about what you think of Mark's choices. Here are some questions to discuss:
   - Why didn't Mark buy the bicycle?
   - How much did the book cost altogether?
   - Why do you think Mark bought his friend an ice cream cone?
   - What charity did Mark give money to?
   - What happened to the money Mark put in the bank?

2. Make your own short cartoon showing what you would do if somebody gave you $10.00.

Advertising

There are examples of advertisements in this section. Decide what the main idea is for each one.

READING HINT

To use money wisely, you need to make sure you only buy things that you really need or want. That's not always easy, because there is a lot of advertising that tries to tell you what to buy.

An advertisement tells you all the good things about a product. It doesn't tell you anything bad!

Advertising is everywhere. The commercials on television are advertisements. You might also see advertisements on posters at the bus shelter, on your computer when you visit a Web site, or on somebody's T-shirt.

▲ How can you tell when you are looking at an advertisement?

Advertising Hooks

A hook is something that catches you and won't let you go. An advertising hook tells you things about a product that might make you think you really, really need it. The problem is that a hook doesn't always tell you the whole truth.

Here are examples of how hooks are used to sell you things. Learn to spot the hooks so you don't get caught!

Hook: This advertisement says you will make friends if you buy the skipping rope.

What do you think? Is buying something new a way to make friends? What is a better way?

Hook: This advertisement says that you get something free.

What do you think? Is the movie pass really free? Or do you pay for it as part of the cost of the burger?

Hook: This advertisement makes Wonderland seem perfect.

What do you think? Are things usually as good as advertisements say they are? Or are they sometimes disappointing?

YOUR TURN

Work with a partner or small group to act out your own television commercial. You could advertise a real product or something you have made up. See how many hooks you can use!

Role-Play or Put on a Skit

In a role play, you pretend you are a real person in a real situation. A skit is like a short play. Part of it can be imaginary. Here's how to make sure you have fun and do a good job.

1. In your group, talk about the scene. Decide
   - who the characters are
   - who will play each character
   - what will happen in the beginning, middle, and end of the scene

2. Your group can now make up the scene as you go along. Or you can write a script. In a script, write down what each character says.

Script for a Commercial

Ravi: I sure feel hot and tired!
Freda: You need PopUp. It's the best soft
         drink in Canada!

---

3. If you are going to present the scene to other people, practise first!

Look again at these pictures and ideas from Chapter 11.
Then decide how you would answer the Big Question:
What do we need to know to use money wisely?

◄ What is something interesting you learned about Canadian money?

▲ How can budgeting help you use money wisely?

◄ What is the main thing you have to remember about advertisements?

CHAPTER 12

IN THE WORLD

The Big Question for this chapter is: *How is Canada connected to the rest of the world?*

You might already know how Canada's heritage connects us to other countries. Many Canadians have family and friends in other parts of the world. This gives us strong connections that we keep through visits, letters, telephone calls, and e-mails.

In this chapter, you can find out about two other ways that Canada is connected to the world. You can read information on
- Canada's location in the world
- how your actions can make a difference to the world's environment

Where Are We?

When you look at the globe on this page and the map on the next page, find continent shapes that are the same in both.

READING HINT

Canada is connected by land and water to other parts of the world. To see these connections, you need to know where Canada is.

The world is round like a ball. A model of the world is called a globe. A globe is one way to show Canada's location in the world.

◄ The world is made up of large areas of land called continents and large areas of water called oceans. How are the continents shown on this globe?

A map is another way to show Canada's location. Turn the page to see where Canada is on a map of the world.

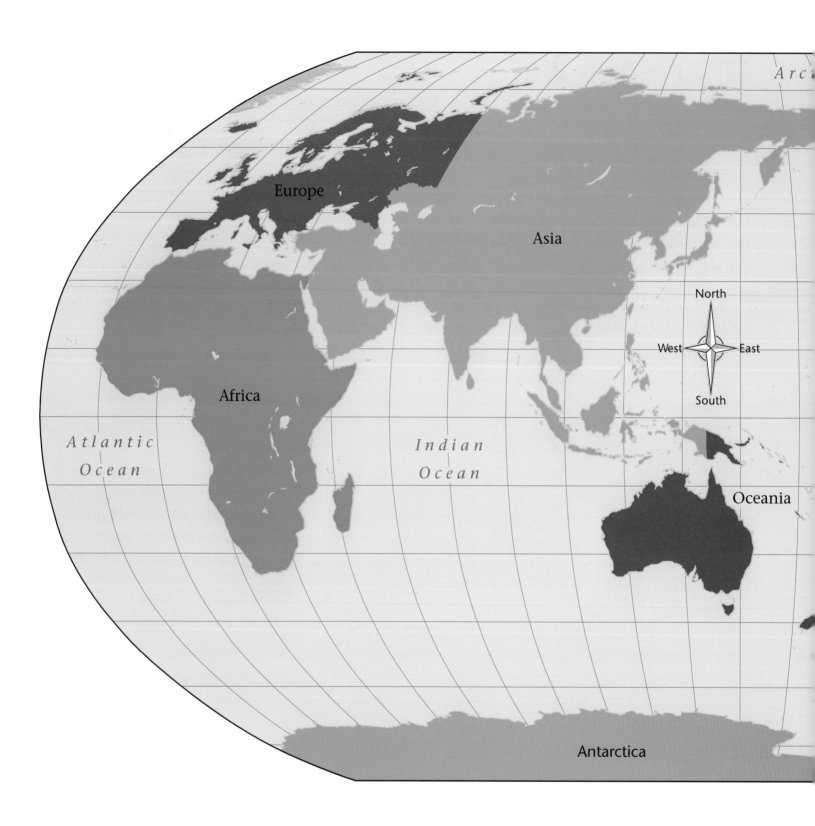

Europe

Asia

Africa

Atlantic
Ocean

Indian
Ocean

North

West ✦ East

South

Oceania

Antarctica

Arc

CANADA

North
America

Pacific Ocean

Atlantic
Ocean

Equator

South
America

Southern Ocean

YOUR TURN

Use the map of the world to answer these questions:
- How many continents are there?
- What is the name of the continent that Canada is part of?
- What three oceans touch Canada?

The Environment

READING HINT

There is a magazine article in this section. Notice the special parts, such as the name of the author, and how the information is organized.

The environment includes land, water, and air. The environment connects Canada to the world because the whole world shares the same water and air.

What happens to the environment in our communities can make a difference to other communities far away.

▲ If we pollute the air, the wind can carry the waste to other continents.

▲ If we pollute the water, the waste can flow down rivers to the oceans. Currents in the oceans can carry it all over the world.

The Good News

Here's the good news: When we take care of the environment in our communities, it is good for the whole world!

In the next three pages, you can read a magazine article about how one school in British Columbia turned an empty field into a garden. Projects like this can help the world's environment.

A GREEN SPACE

BY MARGARET MATTHEWS

If you visit Grandview/ ?Uuqinak'uuh Elementary School in Vancouver, you might be surprised to see a beautiful garden!

Before there was a garden, there was an empty field. The school community decided to turn the field into a green space—a place for plants instead of buildings.

This school has two names! ?Uuqinak'uuh [u-QUIN-ah-cue] means "grand view" in Nuu-chah-nulth.

The empty field was a problem. In wet weather, it was muddy. In dry weather, people walked dogs in the field and didn't clean up the waste.

Why Do We Need Green Spaces?

Green spaces are important to the environment because plants help keep the air clean and make the soil healthy. Green spaces also provide homes for birds, insects, and small animals.

Getting the Job Done

Adults at the school wrote letters to companies and organizations to raise money for plants and gardening equipment.

Garden experts came to the school and talked about different kinds of gardens. Students made garden models and maps to help them decide on a plan for the garden.

Adults and students then worked together to make the garden.

Trucks brought in rich soil. People put the soil in the wooden boxes.

Students helped build large wooden boxes for planting fruit, vegetables, and trees.

These students are planting native plants. These are the kinds of plants that grew in the area before there was a city.

A Success!

Today, the green space at Grandview/?Uuqinak'uuh is growing and doing well. Students volunteer to help weed and plant the garden. Families grow vegetables in the garden.

The garden shows they care for the environment and for each other.

There are many gardens in one at the school: a bird and butterfly garden, food gardens, a native plant garden, a grove of maple trees, and a sandy area for children to play in. There is also an outdoor classroom.

All the people in the school and the community are proud of what they have made. The garden shows they care for the environment and for each other.

Working in the garden is fun!

Is this a school or a garden? It is both!

YOUR TURN

The students and teachers at Grandview/?Uuqinak'uuh Elementary School and other adults worked together to make the world a better place.

Write a report or give a talk that explains what problem they had and how they solved it. Here is an outline you can follow.

Beginning

The problem was:

Middle

The solution they chose was:

The steps they followed were:

End

This is good for the community because . . .

This is good for the whole world because . . .

Look again at these pictures and ideas. Then decide how you would answer the Big Question: *How is Canada connected to the rest of the world?*

◀ What did you already know about Canada's connections to cultures in other parts of the world?

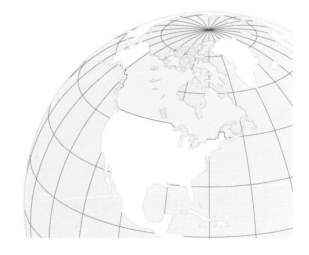

▲ What did you learn about Canada's location in the world?

◀ How can taking care of the environment in our communities help the whole world?

Glossary

Aboriginal peoples
[ab-uh-RIJ-uh-nul] The first people to live in a land.

Canadian citizen
[SIT-ih-zun] A person who is a Canadian. You can become Canadian by being born in Canada, by having a parent who is Canadian, or by taking an oath.

compass rose
[CUM-pas ROZE] The feature on a map that tells you where north, south, east, and west are.

culture
[KUL-chur] The way we live our lives. It includes everyday things, celebrations, and traditions.

diversity
[dih-VERS-ih-tee] Interesting differences.

environment
[en-VYE-run-ment] The land, air, water, weather, plants, and animals in an area. "Environment" can also mean all of these things for the whole world.

government
[GUV-urn-ment] The group of people who are the leaders in a community or a country.

heritage
[HAIR-uh-tij] All the cultures in your family's past. Communities, provinces, and countries also have heritages that are made up of the cultures of all the people who have lived there.

history
[HIS-toh-ree] Everything that happened before today.

legend
[LEJ-und] The part of a map that tells you what the symbols mean. Another meaning of "legend" is a kind of story.

location
[loh-KAY-shun] Where something is.

natural resources
[NACH-uh-rul ree-SORS-ez] The parts of the environment we can use to make the things we need and want.

physical features
[FIZ-i-kul FEE-churz] The landforms and water bodies in an area.

population
[pop-yoo-LAY-shun] The number of people in a place.

responsibilities
[rih-SPON-suh-BIL-ih-teez] Things that you should do to be part of a sharing and caring community.

rights
[RITES] Things you deserve to have and ways you should be treated by others.

scale
[SCAYL] The ruler on a map that tells you how far the distances really are. "Scale" has a lot of other meanings, too. There are scales on fish, scales in music, and scales you weigh things on.

services
[SUR-vis-ez] The things people do to make sure their communities are healthy and safe.

settlers
[SET-lurs] People from other countries who came to live in Canada long ago.

symbol
[SIM-bul] A special shape or line on a map that stands for something such as a landform or water body. A symbol can also be a picture that reminds you of an important idea.

time order
[TIME OR-dur] Organizing information so that the first event is told first, the second event told second, and so on.

traditions
[tra-DIH-shuns] Ideas and ways of doing things that are passed on from adults to children in families and communities.

transportation routes
[trans-por-TAY-shun ROOTZ] Ways to get from one community or place to another.

utilities
[yoo-TIL-ih-teez] Things such as electricity that help make our lives more comfortable.

Index

Acknowledgements

The author and publisher would like to thank Pat Horstead, Principal, Mount Crescent Elementary School, Maple Ridge, BC, for her guidance and advice in developing the manuscript.

The author and publisher would like to thank the following people for reviewing the manuscript:

Donna Anderson
Coal Tyee Elementary School
Nanaimo, BC

Sharon Anderson
David Cameron Elementary School
Victoria, BC

Judy Dallin
Coordinator of Aboriginal Programs
Langley, BC

Maureen Dockendorf, Principal
Blakeburn Elementary School
Coquitlam, BC

Kathleen Gregory
Savory Elementary School
Victoria, BC

Maureen Ciarniello, Elementary Curriculum Consultant
School District #45
West Vancouver, BC

Deborah DeRose, Principal
Beattie Elementary School
Kamloops, BC

Yvonne Mensies, First Nations Curriculum Developer
School District #58
Merritt, BC

Also thanks to the following people who helped in various ways during the development of the manuscript:

Chief Marilyn Gabriel
Phyllis Gabriel
Kwantlen First Nation

Libby Hart, District Principal for Aboriginal Programs
School District #91
Vanderhoof, BC

Illène Pevec
Grandview/?Uuqinak'uuh Elementary School
Vancouver, BC

Hélène Fortin
Citizenship and Immigration Canada

Nicole Michie, Max Jurock, and Nicholas Waizenegger
Students at Blakeburn Elementary School
Coquitlam, BC

Donna Klockars
Literacy Resource Teacher
School District #68
Nanaimo, BC

Lenore Underhill, Elementary Curriculum Consultant
School District #79
Duncan, BC

Jan Wells, Primary Consultant
Vancouver School Board
Vancouver, BC

John Price, Curriculum Consultant
Vancouver School Board
Vancouver, BC

Karla Gamble, Coordinator
Aboriginal Education
BC Ministry of Education
Victoria, BC

The author and publisher would also like to thank the following who helped with specific content areas:

Heritage Branch, Province of British Columbia for pages 52–55; Citizenship and Immigration Canada Welcome Home Campaign for pages 126–127; Sharon Shepherd; Brian Kotila; Kim Moyer; and Seso Bains. The *Encyclopedia of British Columbia*, edited by Daniel Francis, was a much appreciated resource during the writing of this book.

Photo Credits

p. iv   (tl) C. Gupton/First Light, (bl) Patrick Isaac, (tr) © Skjold Photographs, (br) PhotoDisc/ED000818;

p. 1   Corbis/Magma;

p. 3   © Skjold Photographs;

p. 4   © David Young-Wolff/Getty Images/Stone;

p. 8   © Skjold Photographs;

p. 9   Courtesy of Abbotsford City Hall;

p. 11   (tl) © Alec Pytlowany/Masterfile, (bl) Al Harvey/The Slide Farm, (tr) Al Harvey/The Slide Farm, (br) © Daryl Benson/Masterfile;

p. 12   Victoria Times-Colonist – Darren Stone;

p. 16   Photo by Adrian Dorst;

p. 17   (bl) Ian Neill, (tr) Peter Tasker, (br) Rebecca Atleo/Maaqtusiis School;

p. 18   Photo courtesy of the Town of Fort Nelson;

p. 17   (ml) Al Harvey/The Slide Farm, (tr) © Robert Hahn/aaaimagemakers.com, (br) Judith Kenyon/Fort Nelson News;

p. 20   Al Harvey/The Slide Farm;

p. 21   (ml) Andrew Farquhar/VALAN PHOTOS, (tr) Al Harvey/The Slide Farm, (br) Ivy Images;

p. 24   (l) © Alec Pytlowany/Masterfile, (r) Victoria Times-Colonist – Darren Stone;

p. 32   All photos courtesy of Sharon Sterling;

p. 33   All photos courtesy of Sharon Sterling;

p. 34   All photos courtesy of Sharon Sterling;

p. 39   Photo courtesy of Sharon Sterling;

p. 42   Courtesy of the City of Prince George;

p. 43   Courtesy of Phyllis Atkins, Kwantlen First Nation;

p. 47   Courtesy of the City of Kelowna;

p. 49   Patrick Isaac;

p. 50   Courtesy of Phyllis Atkins, Kwantlen First Nation;

p. 51   Al Harvey/The Slide Farm;

p. 52   A-02664/British Columbia Archives;

p. 55   C-05303/British Columbia Archives;

p. 69   Al Harvey/The Slide Farm;

p. 72   G-03799/British Columbia Archives;

p. 73   Vancouver Province – Wayne Leidenfrost;

p. 74   E-00760/British Columbia Archives;

p. 75   © Walter Lanz/aaaimagemakers.com;

p. 77   Al Harvey/The Slide Farm;

p. 78   © Walter Lanz/aaaimagemakers.com;

p. 79   Patrick Isaac;

p. 82   Courtesy of Archie's Greetings and Gifts Ltd.;

p. 83   (tr) CP Picture Archive/Kitchener-Waterloo Record-Rick Koza, (br) Al Harvey/The Slide Farm;

p. 84   (tr) John Eastcott/Yva Momatiuk/VALAN PHOTOS, (br) Photograph by Paul vanPeenen;

p. 85   (tl) © Dave Bartruff/Corbis/Magma, (bl) Jenna Hauck/The Chilliwack Progress;

p. 86   (tr) © Morton Beebe, S.F/Corbis/Magma, (ml) Inter-Cultural Association of Greater Victoria;

p. 87   C. Gupton/First Light;

p. 88   Inter-Cultural Association of Greater Victoria;

p. 89   Corbis/Magma;

p. 91   (mr) Vince Sewell/Vanderhoof Forest District/British Columbia Ministry of Forests; (bl) Courtesy of Ileiren Byles/Vanderhoof Omineca Express;

p. 94   F-09479/British Columbia Archives;

p. 95   Courtesy of Ileiren Byles/Vanderhoof Omineca Express;

p. 96   NA-10262/British Columbia Archives;

p. 97   All photos courtesy of Ileiren Byles/Vanderhoof Omineca Express;

p. 99   Courtesy of Ileiren Byles/Vanderhoof Omineca Express;

p. 100   CP Picture Archive/Andrew Vaughan;

p. 106   J. R. Page/VALAN PHOTOS;

p. 107   (tr) D. Nunuk/First Light, (bl) Ivy Images;

p. 108   L. MacDougal/First Light;

p. 109   (tr) © J. A. Kraulis/Masterfile, (bl) © J. A. Kraulis/Masterfile;

p. 110   Picture Finders Ltd./Firstlight.ca ;

p. 111   (tl) Bill Ivy, (bl), Herman H. Giethoorn/VALAN PHOTOS;

p. 112   Barrett & MacKay;

p. 113   (tr) Al Harvey/The Slide Farm, (bl) J. Sylvester/First Light;

p. 114   S. J. Krasemann/VALAN PHOTOS;

p. 115   (tr) Phil Hoffman/Lone Pine Photo, (bl) © Dan Guravich/Corbis/Magma,

p. 119   CP Picture Archive/Ryan Remiorz;

p. 120   © Bill Brooks/Masterfile;

p. 125   CP Picture Archive/Aaron Harris;

p. 126   Drawing courtesy of Citizenship and Immigration Canada Welcome Home Campaign (www.cic.gc.ca/welcomehome);

p. 128   © Bill Brooks/Masterfile;

p. 129   Boris Spremo/Magma;

p. 130   All photos P. Joiner;

p. 131   (tr) Bettmann Corbis/Magma, (m) Pierre-Paul Poulin/Magma;

p. 135   Dick Hemingway;

p. 139   P. Joiner;

p. 145   Photo courtesy of Illène Pevec;

p. 146   All photos courtesy of Illène Pevec;

p. 147   All photos courtesy of Illène Pevec;

p. 149   (tl) Courtesy of Archie's Greetings and Gifts Ltd., (br) Courtesy of Illène Pevec;

p. 156   Courtesy of Peter Owens/British Columbia Teacher's Federation.

Every effort has been made to trace the original source of material and photographs contained in this book. Where the attempt has been unsuccessful, the publisher would be pleased to hear from copyright holders to rectify any omissions.

About the Cover

The picture on the front cover of this textbook shows a quilt made by students and adult helpers at Blakeburn Elementary School in Coquitlam, British Columbia. They made this quilt to show the diversity in their community.

Each student used fabric paint to make a self-portrait on a square of material. Adult helpers and students then worked together to sew the squares into a large quilt.

The quilt now hangs on the wall in the entrance to the school. It is a reminder to everyone who comes in that Blakeburn Elementary is a caring and sharing place!

▲ This photograph shows student Cindy Lui and Blakeburn's artist-in-residence, Wendy Louington-Coulter, working on the quilt.